# MIXED EMOTIONS

BY RICHARD BAER

★

★

DRAMATISTS
PLAY SERVICE
INC.

Photo by Martha Swope

The set from the Broadway production of "Mixed Emotions." Set design by Neil Peter Jampolis.

MIXED EMOTIONS received its Broadway premiere (Michael Maurer, Producer), at the Golden Theatre in New York City, on October 12, 1993. It was directed by Tony Giordano; the set and lighting designs were by Neil Peter Jampolis; the costume design was by David Murin; the sound design was by Dan Moses Schreier; the dance consultant was Christopher Daniels and the production stage manager was Tom Aberger. The cast was as follows:

CHUCK ..................................................................... Vinny Capone
RALPH ........................................................................ Brian Smiar
CHRISTINE MILLMAN .............................. Katherine Helmond
HERMAN LEWIS ...................................................... Harold Gould

MIXED EMOTIONS was produced under the title EMBRACE-ABLE YOU in Los Angeles, California (directed by Tom Troupe), Toronto, Canada and Kansas City, Missouri (directed by Reva Stern). In these productions the lead roles of Christine and Herman were played by Jacqueline Scott and Tom Troupe.

MIXED EMOTIONS was produced in Chicago, Illinois. It was directed by Reva Stern. The lead roles of Christine and Herman were played by Betsy Palmer and Tom Troupe.

# CAST OF CHARACTERS
(In Order of Appearance)

RALPH
CHUCK
CHRISTINE MILLMAN
HERMAN LEWIS

# SETTING

The living room of Christine's apartment, Manhattan.

**ACT ONE**
Scene 1 — Thursday afternoon.
Scene 2 — Thursday, early evening.
Scene 3 — Thursday night.

**ACT TWO**
Friday morning.

# MIXED EMOTIONS

## ACT ONE

### Scene 1

*Time: This February. Thursday afternoon.*

*Place: Manhattan. The living room and elevated entry hall of Christine's apartment, on Central Park West, with a view of the East Side skyline. Along the walls are bookcases with built-in stereo, bar, refrigerator, and a gas fireplace. The elegant furniture includes a sofa, an armchair with ottoman, and a large area rug.*

*At rise: Room unoccupied, until from off-stage bedroom wing come Ralph and Chuck, two Mayflower moving men, in matching jumpsuits with name logos on them. Each man carries two empty Mayflower book cartons; Ralph also carries a sheaf of wrapping paper. Ralph is in his 50s, Chuck in his early 20s. They descend to living room.*

RALPH.    I'll pack the fragile stuff, you pack books and records. *(They cross to opposite bookcases, set down cartons, Ralph carefully placing them, Chuck dropping them at random. As Ralph begins to take framed photos, bric-a-brac, and objets d'art from shelves, deftly and swiftly wrap them in paper and put them in a carton, Chuck looks at shelves bearing books and compact discs.)*
CHUCK.    I'm surprised Mrs. what's-her-name has such lousy taste in music.
RALPH.    Her name isn't Mrs. what's-her-name; it's Mrs. Millman. How many times did I tell you to always make it your business to learn the client's name?

CHUCK.    Ten thousand times. But you never told me why. After we unload them do we ever see them again? *(He tosses the CDs into a carton. The noise this makes prompts Ralph to stop working, whirl, and watch Chuck toss in two more CDs.)*
RALPH.    Chuck, don't throw them. Deposit them. Gently, lovingly. *(Chuck gets another CD, kisses it, then mincingly puts it in carton.)* That's perfect, except cut the kiss and don't pack one at a time. *(Chuck takes down four CDs, looks at their titles.)*
CHUCK.    Ralph, listen to this. *(Reading, derisively.)* "La Bo-he-me." "Por-gee and Bess." "Ray-vel's Bowler-O." *(Into entry hall, from off-stage kitchen wing, comes Christine Millman, age 61, gorgeous, sensible, unpretentious. She's dressed smartly but casually, since she's in the throes of moving preparations. She appears in time to hear Chuck read fourth CD title.)* "A Stereo Stroll Down Memory Lane."
CHRISTINE.    Chuck, don't pack that. I'd like to listen to it.
CHUCK.    Before me and Ralph leave or after?
CHRISTINE.    After. On the wild theory I'll have time to stop packing cartons and sit down. *(Chuck crosses to return CD to its shelf, as the entry hall intercom buzzes. Christine goes to phone, lifts receiver, converses with the lobby doorman.)* Yes?... You're kidding.... Don't move your lips; talk like a ventriloquist .... Oh. Well, if he already heard you, you can't say I'm not home, so I guess my only choice is: Send him up. *(She hangs up, descends to living room, saying.)* Fellas, I regret to say I have a visitor. So both of you take over for me in the kitchen ... I'll get rid of him as soon as I can, and when the coast is clear I'll come in and tell you. *(Movers ascend to entry, exit to kitchen wing. Christine eyes a dish of chocolates on the coffee table, takes a chocolate, eats it, then consumes a second, then, surrendering to gluttony, a third, as front door chimes sound. Christine starts for door, notices three sample carpet swatches on sofa, and hides them behind a cushion. Door chimes sound again. She ascends to entry hall, unbolts door, opens it. In trudges Herman Lewis, 65, in overcoat, fake fur Russian hat, muffler, gloves, and galoshes in which are tucked the trousers of his business suit. Herman is a shrewd, blunt, self-made man who can be, simultaneously, exasperating and endearing.)* Hello, Herman. What an unexpected surprise.

HERMAN.   Where were you?

CHRISTINE.   Where was I when?

HERMAN.   This afternoon. At three o'clock.

CHRISTINE.   I was in my kitchen, packing my dishes.

HERMAN.   Why weren't you in Long Island, at your husband's cemetery?

CHRISTINE.   What for?

HERMAN.   To pay your respects to him.

CHRISTINE.   I did that yesterday.

HERMAN.   Yesterday. Why yesterday?

CHRISTINE.   Because a year ago yesterday was when he died.

HERMAN.   Wrong. He died a year ago today.

CHRISTINE.   He died a year ago yesterday.

HERMAN.   Then why did you call me last Sunday and invite me to join you at your husband's grave at three o'clock this Thursday?

CHRISTINE.   I invited you to join me at three o'clock this Wednesday.

HERMAN.   You said Thursday. I wrote it down in my date book.

CHRISTINE.   I don't care where you wrote it — I said Wednesday.

HERMAN.   You said Thursday. Today. When for a fifty-six dollar round trip cab fare I had the pleasure of grieving all alone, in a blinding snowstorm.

CHRISTINE.   Herman, I said, slowly and clearly, Wednesday, February fourth.

HERMAN.   Aha! You just trapped yourself. Moe died on February fifth.

CHRISTINE.   No he didn't. He died on February fourth.

HERMAN.   Christine, are you telling me I don't know when my best friend died?

CHRISTINE.   Are you telling me I don't know when my husband died?

HERMAN.   Yes, I am. Go check the certificate. I'll wait. *(He descends to living room, sits on sofa, as Christine closes front door, then descends to living room.)*

7

CHRISTINE.    If you don't believe me, ask my daughters, both of whom, and their husbands, were with me at the cemetery, yesterday, Wednesday, February fourth.

HERMAN.    Oh. How much did the cab cost?

CHRISTINE.    We went in Joan and Larry's car. Because last Sunday I told you to meet us at their apartment so we could all drive out together. Then when you didn't show up I called your secretary to find out where you were, and she said you were on the way to a major fight with your accountant.

HERMAN.    Did you try to reach me at his office?

CHRISTINE.    No. I was very hurt that fighting with your accountant took precedence over honoring the memory of your best friend. *(Crossing to shelves Chuck worked at.)* Herman, excuse me, but I have a lot of packing to do, so with your kind permission I'll do it. *(She proceeds to pack books, while Herman fans his forehead.)*

HERMAN.    Why do you keep this room so hot?

CHRISTINE.    I'm sorry. I can either turn on the air conditioner, or you can take off your snowsuit.

HERMAN.    I forgot I had it on. *(He rises, removes gloves, coat, hat, and muffler, puts them on ottoman, during.)* Christine, permit me to point out that by the same token that *you* were hurt, *I'm* hurt that you thought anything could stop me from being at that cemetery unless, as the evidence seems to indicate, I was at the right place at the wrong time. *(He sits on sofa, removes galoshes.)* I'm also hurt that you didn't call to find out why I failed to appear. For all you knew I could've suddenly followed in your husband's footsteps.

CHRISTINE.    I *did* call. Last night. Your line was busy.

HERMAN.    It could've been the paramedics, calling the coroner.

CHRISTINE.    Would that tie up the phone for two hours?

HERMAN.    No. I was continuing my fight with my accountant. But you could've told the operator to cut in for an emergency.

CHRISTINE.    I had her verify there was conversation — from which I cleverly deduced that if you were on the phone you were alive.

8

HERMAN.    Let me know when you're tired of picking on me. Getting picked on is not the reason I came here.

CHRISTINE.    What is?

HERMAN.    I came to cheer you up. To take your mind off the horrible tragedy of Moe's death.

CHRISTINE.    That's very thoughtful of you.

HERMAN.    Especially in a blinding snowstorm.

CHRISTINE.    However, I don't need cheering up. I'm not depressed.

HERMAN.    Why not? Don't you miss him?

CHRISTINE.    Of course I do. And yesterday I was depressed. But last night I went out to dinner with my family ... we toasted Moe's memory ... we went around the table, each of us describing one of his fine qualities ... we all realized how much he meant to us ... but life must go on ... and I got over my depression.

HERMAN.    Completely?

CHRISTINE.    No. Does anyone ever get over the loss of a husband, or a wife, completely? Miriam's been gone three years. Are you completely over losing her?

HERMAN.    I'm trying. *(Beat.)* What restaurant did you go to?

CHRISTINE.    A little Italian place, on Second Avenue. Alberto's, or Umberto's, or something berto's. Larry chose it.

HERMAN.    Who paid?

CHRISTINE.    Paul and Larry split it.

HERMAN.    If I'd've been there *I* would've paid.

CHRISTINE.    If you'd've been at the cemetery you'd've been there. *(After a pause, wistfully.)* You know what would be nice?

HERMAN.    If I send a check to Paul and Larry?

CHRISTINE.    No. If last night, up there ... Moe and Miriam had dinner together.

HERMAN.    Well, if they did, let's hope it wasn't at her apartment, so he didn't have to eat her cooking.

CHRISTINE.    Herman, with all due respect, that's a rotten thing to say.

HERMAN.    It's true. My wife had many virtues — but two things she never was noted for were parachute jumping and cooking.

9

CHRISTINE. I think she was an excellent cook.

HERMAN. You do?

CHRISTINE. Yes. I do.

HERMAN. In that case, as her frequent dinner guest for more than thirty years, name me one item that was personally cooked by Miriam — not by a caterer, by Miriam — name me one item that you consider edible.

CHRISTINE. *(Upon reflection.)* Broiled chicken.

HERMAN. Possibly. Anything else?

CHRISTINE. *(More reflection, then.)* She made an interesting meatloaf.

HERMAN. The topic is "edible," not "interesting."

CHRISTINE. Then let's change the topic! Why can't you let Miriam's cooking, and Miriam, rest in peace?

HERMAN. I can, and I will.

CHRISTINE. Thank you.

HERMAN. Except to say that I strongly doubt that Miriam and Moe even *see* each other *(Pointing upward.)* up there. Because I strongly doubt that up there even exists. In case you never noticed, I'm not a devout Catholic.

CHRISTINE. Neither am I. As I told you all nine thousand times you teased me about it, I quit being devout when I got married.

HERMAN. But every now and then doesn't it sneak up on you? Like when you're walking up Fifth Avenue, on route to Sak's, or Bergdorf's, and you come to St. Patrick's Cathedral. Don't you ever duck inside and light a candle? *(Christine picks up the candy dish.)*

CHRISTINE. Would you care for a chocolate?

HERMAN. No thanks, all I'd care for is an answer to my question. *(She takes a piece of candy, eats it, sets down dish.)* Do you or don't you ever duck inside and light a candle?

CHRISTINE. I do. But very infrequently.

HERMAN. How infrequently?

CHRISTINE. Two or three times a year.

HERMAN. Closer to two, or closer to three?

CHRISTINE. Closer to three. But only since Moe died.

HERMAN. And each time, how many candles do you light?

CHRISTINE.    Four. One for my mother, one for my father, one for Moe, and one for Miriam.

HERMAN.    So counting each candle as a separate religious experience ... four candles three times per year adds up to twelve candles per year, or one candle per month. And the total should really be doubled.

CHRISTINE.    Why?

HERMAN.    Because lighting Catholic candles for Jews is burning the candle at both ends.

CHRISTINE.    *(Wearily.)* Herman, go home. It's been nice chatting with you, but I'm very, very, very busy, so thanks for coming and go home.

HERMAN.    Aren't you even going to offer me a glass of water?

CHRISTINE.    No. I offered you chocolate, and you rejected me. *(Herman reaches over, takes a chocolate, eats it.)*

HERMAN.    There. Now if only I had something to wash it down.

CHRISTINE.    Herman, may I offer you a glass of water?

HERMAN.    I accept. *(Christine ascends to entry hall. Herman calls.)* Unless you happen to have Diet Pepsi. *(Christine returns, crosses to bar's refrigerator, takes out a beverage bottle, opens it.)*

CHRISTINE.    Do you take your Diet Pepsi with ice or without?

HERMAN.    Was it in the refrigerator?

CHRISTINE.    Yes.

HERMAN.    How long?

CHRISTINE.    A week, two weeks — I don't keep formal inventory.

HERMAN.    If you store soft drinks too long they lose their fizz. *(Christine pours cola into a glass, and reports.)*

CHRISTINE.    It didn't lose its fizz. It's fizzing superbly.

HERMAN.    Then why weaken its flavor with ice? *(She sets down the bottle, shuts refrigerator, carries glass to Herman, gives it to him.)* Thanks.

CHRISTINE.    You're welcome. *(He sets glass on table.)* Aren't you going to drink it?

HERMAN.    First I let it breathe. *(Christine packs more books.)*

Well, are you excited?

CHRISTINE.    About what?

HERMAN.    Moving to Florida, and sharing a condominium with a wonderful woman like Beverly Siegel.

CHRISTINE.    Yes, I'm excited. So is she. I'm lonely without Moe; she's lonely without Arnold. *(Stops packing.)* Herman, will you please do me a favor?

HERMAN.    What?

CHRISTINE.    *(Re: his cola.)* Drink. If it loses its fizz I'll never forgive myself. *(Herman takes a sip, then springs to his feet.)*

HERMAN.    Hold everything!

CHRISTINE.    What's wrong?

HERMAN.    This isn't Diet Pepsi. It's Diet Coke.

CHRISTINE.    *(Feigning dread.)* Oh my God, he caught me! *(He strides to bar, sets down glass, picks up empty bottle, displays it.)*

HERMAN.    See? It doesn't say Diet Pepsi; it says Diet Coke.

CHRISTINE.    Fool that I am, I thought I could get away with it.

HERMAN.    No chance. Most people can't tell the difference, but I can. I have very sensitive taste buds.

CHRISTINE.    I'm sorry. Can you ever forgive me, or did I seal my doom?

HERMAN.    That depends on what other diet beverages you've got. *(Christine crosses, opens refrigerator, looks inside.)*

CHRISTINE.    I have club soda ... and club soda.

HERMAN.    Club soda. *(Christine extracts the bottle, closes refrigerator, gets a clean glass.)* Nobody ever accused me of being difficult. *(She opens can, fills glass.)*

CHRISTINE.    Yippee! It's fizzing like hotcakes. To celebrate, I'll drink the Diet Coke. *(She sets down bottle, gives him the soda, picks up the cola, and they exchange toasts.)*

HERMAN.    To the memory of Moe Millman.

CHRISTINE.    And the memory of Miriam Lewis. *(They clink glasses, sip their drinks, then Christine goes to bookcase, sets glass on a shelf, packs more books.)*

HERMAN.    Last night, at the restaurant, when everybody described Moe's fine qualities, what'd *you* say?

CHRISTINE.    I said he was kind, gentle, and considerate.

HERMAN. If I was there, *I* would've said his finest quality was something else.
CHRISTINE. What?
HERMAN. His warmth. He had more warmth than any coat he ever sold. I loved him like a brother.
CHRISTINE. He loved you too. And he loved Miriam. And so did I. *(She resumes packing; he crosses to her.)*
HERMAN. So it looks like you're moving to Florida.
CHRISTINE. Yep, that's what it looks like.
HERMAN. When do the movers come?
CHRISTINE. They're already here.
HERMAN. They're here? Where?
CHRISTINE. In the kitchen. They're supposed to be packing my books, but they can't, because I'm having company. *(She packs more books.)*
HERMAN. When do the movers with the moving van show up?
CHRISTINE. Tomorrow morning, eight A.M. But they're the same movers. If you'd like to meet them before you leave, I'll call them in right now.
HERMAN. Don't bother. You're paying them to work, not to socialize. *(Beat.)* So in other words, the movers leave tomorrow and you leave Saturday.
CHRISTINE. Half right, half wrong. The movers leave tomorrow, and so do I. From Kennedy Airport, at five-fifteen P.M.
HERMAN. Tomorrow? You told me you leave Saturday.
CHRISTINE. No I didn't.
HERMAN. Christine, explain something to me. Unless Beverly has two living rooms and two dining rooms and six bedrooms, how can all the furniture in your apartment fit in her apartment?
CHRISTINE. It can't. That's why I'm putting my furniture in storage, and all I'm sending to Florida is clothes, books, records, and prized possessions.
HERMAN. I didn't know that.
CHRISTINE. I told you the last time I saw you in person, January first, at Joan and Larry's New Year's party.

HERMAN.   All you said at that party was you were thinking of selling your apartment.

CHRISTINE.   I said I sold it. I said I was thinking of selling it the *next* to last time I saw you. At Paul and Barbara's. On Thanksgiving. *(Carton full, she packs another.)*

HERMAN.   Won't you miss the furniture that you and Moe invested so much sentimental value in?

CHRISTINE.   I'm being practical. Bev's apartment is furnished fully and magnificently. She used a magnificent decorator. Me.

HERMAN.   Is her carpeting equally magnificent?

CHRISTINE.   Almost.

HERMAN.   And *that*, if memory serves, you got from me. At cost.

CHRISTINE.   Plus twelve percent.

HERMAN.   Eleven. *(After sipping his drink.)* I presume Bev lined up lots of clients for you.

CHRISTINE.   She's trying.

HERMAN.   She'll succeed. When she throws her two hundred pounds around, she can do anything.

CHRISTINE.   Two hundred? She's one fifteen, or tops, one twenty.

HERMAN.   I added the weight of her makeup and jewelry.

CHRISTINE.   Untrue, and unkind. She may be slightly ... over-stated, but she's more fun to be with than anyone I know — present company excluded.

HERMAN.   She's also the world's leading non-stop talker. Rumor has it that when Arnold wisely died, Beverly talked to him five days before she noticed he wasn't showing any interest. *(He sits on sofa, puts glass on coffee table. Christine takes an art book from its shelf, looks at its title.)*

CHRISTINE.   *Art Treasures of the Louvre Museum.* Remember where this came from?

HERMAN.   No. Where?

CHRISTINE.   From the Louvre Museum. Miriam bought it for me on the last vacation the four of us took together. *(She sits beside him, flips pages, and waxes nostalgic.)* Twenty-six glorious days. In England ... Ireland ... Scotland ... France ... Italy

14

... Spain ... Portugal ... Norway ... Denmark ... Sweden ... Switzerland ... and Israel.

HERMAN.    And I thought we were spreading ourselves too thin.

CHRISTINE.    But we weren't, thanks to Miriam. She studied guide books, she planned each day in advance, so we saw everything worth seeing and did everything worth doing.

HERMAN.    Remember that time in Rome? At the Vatican? When the four of us stood in the parking lot waiting for the Pope to come out on his balcony and wave hello.

CHRISTINE.    It wasn't a parking lot, it was St. Peter's Square. There must've been ten thousand people.

HERMAN.    You, of course, were in your element. But Moe and Miriam and me were like three misplaced matzoh balls.

CHRISTINE.    Then the Pope came out on the balcony and went like this. *(She makes three arm gestures, to her left, her center, and her right.)* Miriam said, "Christine, what does that mean?" And before I could answer, you said it means: *(Repeating arm gestures.)* "I want the three Jewish people to get off my private property." *(Nostalgia ended, Christine rises, puts book in carton, packs others. Herman rises, crosses to her.)*

HERMAN.    Let's say you *do* find clients in Florida. What about your business sources? All of them are here.

CHRISTINE.    And I'll order from them. And I'll develop sources there.

HERMAN.    Including for carpeting?

CHRISTINE.    No. I promise all my carpeting will come from you.

HERMAN.    Good. Then I guess all you'll have to worry about is how happy you can be living two thousand miles away from your children and grandchildren.

CHRISTINE.    The distance from New York City to Miami is one thousand and ninety miles. The flying time is two hours and thirty-eight minutes. I'll still be able to visit my family, and they'll still be able to visit me.

HERMAN.    I hope you have the energy to show them a good time.

CHRISTINE.    Why shouldn't I have the energy?

HERMAN. You'll be exhausted from floundering like a fish out of water. You're a native New Yorker. Once a native New Yorker, always a native New Yorker.

CHRISTINE. Bev was a native New Yorker. She's not floundering.

HERMAN. You're not Bev. Bev can swim anywhere. She's a barracuda.

CHRISTINE. Your son was a native New Yorker. Is he floundering?

HERMAN. He's not in Florida; he's in California.

CHRISTINE. And is he happy or unhappy?

HERMAN. He's happy. He's got everything he every wanted. A house with a tennis court ... a Mercedes-Benz convertible ... two beautiful children ... two beautiful ex-wives.

CHRISTINE. You omitted his thriving practice.

HERMAN. All orthopedic surgeons thrive in California. Between the tennis and the skiing and the surfing and the drunken driving, the whole state is a mass of broken bones. *(Christine gets her glass, sips cola, then.)*

CHRISTINE. Herman, I have a question for you.

HERMAN. If it's can I stay for dinner, the answer is yes.

CHRISTINE. I'm sorry, but the movers are working until eight o'clock, and I'll probably be working till at least ten.

HERMAN. Don't over-exert yourself. Every few minutes take a break to look at the majestic New York skyline. *(Pointing toward windows.)* You'll never see a sight like that anyplace else on earth.

CHRISTINE. That leads me to my question.

HERMAN. And at night, it's a glittering diamond necklace that not even Beverly Siegel could afford.

CHRISTINE. I'll try again. That leads me to my question.

HERMAN. As always, you have my undivided attention. *(He sits on sofa. Christine sets her glass on coffee table.)*

CHRISTINE. Since there's about to be a big change in my life, and since I made it clear I hope it's a change for the better, and since you and I have known each other more than thirty years, and although we don't always see eye to eye, I like to believe you have a certain degree of respect for my ability, and for my *right* to make my own decisions, and since my decision is to move to Florida ... and here comes the question.... Don't you think it might be appropriate for you to *support* my decision, and wish me luck, and stop being such a kvetch?

HERMAN. I'm glad you asked that, because I have an excellent answer. *(He reaches toward his inner jacket pocket, and knocks over the cushion behind which Christine put the three carpet swatches. He picks them up.)* What are these?

CHRISTINE. Cocktail napkins.

HERMAN. To me they look like carpet samples. *(Reading their identification tags.)* They *are* carpet samples. And according to the tag, this one is from a dealer named Gotham Carpets. And so is this one. And so is this one.

CHRISTINE. Are you trying to make me feel guilty?

HERMAN. Guilty? Why? Merely because none of the tags on none of the samples happen to say Herman Lewis Floor Coverings, Incorporated? *(Receiving no reply, he rises, and "supportively" assures.)* Christine, it's a free country. You've got every right to trade with firms who haven't known you practically all of your adult life and who weren't your husband's best friend, so please, under no circumstances, don't feel guilty.

CHRISTINE. I don't.

HERMAN. *(Brandishing samples.)* Then why did you hide them from me?

CHRISTINE. I didn't hide them. I just put them where I hoped you wouldn't find them.

HERMAN. Why?

CHRISTINE. To avoid bruising your delicate ego.

HERMAN. You didn't. You only amused it, because these are three of the most laughable samples I've ever seen. *(He tosses them on coffee table.)*

CHRISTINE. Then the laugh is on you, because, for your information, Herman Lewis Floor Coverings carries the exact same lines.

HERMAN. Only two of them. The apricot we discontinued.

CHRISTINE. And ha ha ha — the apricot is what Bev

chose. *(She realizes she blundered, and she pays the price.)*

HERMAN.    Bev? Bev Siegel? You're buying carpet from Gotham Carpets for a condominium that *you're* going to live in?

CHRISTINE.    It's only for the powder room. She insists I order it from Gotham in tribute to Arnold. His nephew works there.

HERMAN.    So when you promised you'd buy all your carpeting from me ...

CHRISTINE.    I lied. *(Picking up her glass.)* I also lied about the Diet Pepsi. I gave you Diet Coke on purpose — and to trick your taste buds, I slipped in arsenic. *(She drinks what's left of the cola chug-a-lug.)* Farewell, Herman. I no longer deserve to live. *(She sets down glass, falls into the armchair, rigidly thrusts out her legs, closes her eyes, plays dead.)*

HERMAN.    Christine.

CHRISTINE.    Too late. I'm already up there. *(Darting one arm upward.)* Hi, Moe. Hi, Miriam. *(She lowers arm, sits inert.)*

HERMAN.    Christine. *(She doesn't respond. He inquires.)* Christine, will you marry me? *(Christine opens her eyes, otherwise not moving.)*

CHRISTINE.    Will I what?

HERMAN.    Will you marry me? *(She sits normally.)*

CHRISTINE.    Congratulations, Herman. You really know how to wake the dead.

HERMAN.    I was looking for a way to lead into it a bit more gracefully, but I couldn't find one. So will you marry me?

CHRISTINE.    *(Incredulously.)* Will I marry you? Will I marry you?

HERMAN.    That's the general drift of the question, yes.

CHRISTINE.    Herman, be serious. You're not serious. Are you serious?

HERMAN.    If I wasn't, would I come here in a blinding snowstorm, and run the risk of not finding a taxi when I leave?

CHRISTINE.    Oh my God, you're serious!

HERMAN.    I think it's the logical move for both of us.

CHRISTINE. Why? (*From his inner jacket pocket Herman takes reading glasses and a folded sheet of paper. He puts on glasses, unfolds paper, and refers to what he wrote on it.*)

HERMAN. Number one:

CHRISTINE. You made a list?

HERMAN. That's correct. Four reasons why we should get married.

CHRISTINE. When did you make a list?

HERMAN. Last night, after I surrendered to my accountant. But I've been toying with the concept for the past three months.

CHRISTINE. Why didn't you tell me? You had plenty of opportunity. In the past three months we've been constant companions. Once in November and once in January.

HERMAN. I was keeping a low profile. Until I was totally positive that my logic has no flaws in it. Which it doesn't. For the following reasons. (*Looking at list.*) Number one:

CHRISTINE. Herman, don't do this! Please, don't do this. I'm very flattered — but not only would it not be logical for us to get married, it would be insane.

HERMAN. At least do me the courtesy of listening with an open mind.

CHRISTINE. But my answer will still be no.

HERMAN. Then do me the courtesy of listening with a closed mind. (*She sighs in resignation. He looks at list, speaks as if proposing a business deal.*) Number one: The economic factor. Two can live cheaper than one. If you live with me, in my apartment, I won't charge you any rent. Plus there'll only be one phone bill, one electric bill, and one gas bill. We'll also save money on things like cereal and toothpaste by buying the large economy family size.

CHRISTINE. Am I allowed to ask questions, or make comments?

HERMAN. Certainly.

CHRISTINE. Number one on *some* lists is: "I'm madly in love with you."

HERMAN. I cover that aspect of the situation under ...

*(Consulting list.)* Number three. Also under number four.

CHRISTINE.    When Moe proposed to me, love was number one. Wasn't it number one when you proposed to Miriam?

HERMAN.    I don't remember.

CHRISTINE.    I bet it was.

HERMAN.    You might very well be right. But when I proposed to Miriam I didn't have a nickel to my name, so I placed the economic factor way down at the bottom.

CHRISTINE.    *(To get on with it.)* What's number two?

HERMAN.    *(Consulting list.)* Number two:  The age factor. That covers the point that neither of us is a spring chicken. I'm sixty-five; you're sixty-three.

CHRISTINE.    *(Taken aback.)* No I'm not.

HERMAN.    *(Surprised.)* You're not? How old are you?

CHRISTINE.    Sixty-one. Who told you I'm sixty-three?

HERMAN.    Nobody. But if Miriam was alive that's what she'd be — and I always thought you were the same age.

CHRISTINE.    Well, we weren't. I was two years younger.

HERMAN.    *(Not fully convinced.)*  Be that as it may … *(Reading from notes.)* Anyone who's sixty-three or older —

CHRISTINE.    *(Interrupting.)* Sixty-one.

HERMAN.    Excuse me. I wrote sixty-three.

CHRISTINE.    Erase it.

HERMAN.    *(Revising his "text.")* Anyone who's sixty-one or older has no way of knowing how much time the future holds in store. So it's to our mutual benefit to grab each other while the grabbing's good.

CHRISTINE.    What's number three?

HERMAN.    Number three:  The period of adjustment factor. You and I have known each other for more than thirty years — so we won't be newlyweds who only know each other on the surface, and after the wedding it takes them months, or years, to learn what really makes the other *(After turning to back of page, where the sentence is completed.)* person tick. *(Beat.)* Number four:

CHRISTINE.    Not so fast! You said number three discusses love.

HERMAN.    It does. My specific note to myself is:  *(Reading.)* When two people have held warm affection for each other for as long as we have, warm affection can blossom into love. *(Looking at her.)* But due to your negative attitude I left that out. *(She rises, crosses to him.)*
CHRISTINE.    I *do* hold warm affection for you. But there's a large leap from holding affection and ... and ... and ...
HERMAN.    Desiring to share my bed?
CHRISTINE.    Yes. To be perfectly honest ... *(She sits on sofa, touches the empty cola glass.)* I even felt squeamish about drinking from your glass. *(Undaunted, he sits beside her.)*
HERMAN.    Number four:  The physical factor. By that I mean that I possess normal biological urges in the area of sex.
CHRISTINE.    Herman, if I may be so bold, at your age — define "normal."
HERMAN.    I want more than I get.
CHRISTINE.    That's a very clear definition.
HERMAN.    I used it before I got married. And after.
CHRISTINE.    I know. Miriam told me.
HERMAN.    She told you what?
CHRISTINE.    She said you were always ... strongly motivated.
HERMAN.    I was, and I'm proud to say, I am. *(Beat.)* What else did she say?
CHRISTINE.    She said you were an excellent dancer. And you were. I wished *Moe* could dance like you. I often said "Moe, if you could dance like Herman, the world would be your oyster."
HERMAN.    I meant what else did she say about her sex life?
CHRISTINE.    *(After a pause.)* Nothing.
HERMAN.    I don't believe you. I think you think she can hear us ... *(Pointing upward.)* up there ... and you don't want to embarrass her.
CHRISTINE.    Embarrass *her*? I don't want to embarrass *you*.
HERMAN.    Try. The odds are all against you, but try.
CHRISTINE.    All right, if you insist ... the only other thing she said about her sex life was ... each and every time that you were in the mood ... you said:  *(In macho tones.)* "Sweet-

heart, are you ready for a visit from the big guy?"

HERMAN.    I can't believe she told you.

CHRISTINE.    Are you embarrassed?

HERMAN.    Slightly.

CHRISTINE.    Why only slightly?

HERMAN.    I never said it in that tone of voice. I always said it much more romantically.

CHRISTINE.    Miriam must've been afraid it might ruin my marriage, because I couldn't make her tell me how big the big guy really is.

HERMAN.    Look it up. It's in the *Guiness Book of Records.*

CHRISTINE.    I guess Moe saw it, in men's rooms all over the world, but when I asked him if there was anything about you that he was jealous of, he said yes, your dancing.

HERMAN.    Christine, can we kindly not pursue this? At the moment all I'm offering you is my hand. *(Consulting list.)* I assume that you have normal biological urges too, and that your urges, like mine, currently find themselves all dressed up with no place to go. Therefore ... this part I memorized. *(Taking her hand.)* Christine, I think you're a very terrific person, and I'd be grateful and honored if you would be my wife. *(Releasing her hand.)* That concludes my formal sales pitch. *(He folds the paper, removes his glasses, pockets both. Christine leans over, kisses his cheek.)* Should I take that as a sign of being sold?

CHRISTINE.    *(Softly, earnestly.)* It's a sign that I'm grateful and honored to be — and I hope to stay — your friend.

HERMAN.    But you won't marry me.

CHRISTINE.    I can't. *(Herman rises, starts to put on his muffler, overcoat, and hat.)*

HERMAN.    I'll be out of here in less than fifteen seconds. *(Christine rises, crosses to him, reasons.)*

CHRISTINE.    Herman, how can I marry you? How can you marry me? *(He gets his galoshes, starts to put them on, but doesn't fasten them.)* It wouldn't work. I'd always think of you as Miriam's husband; you'd always think of me as Moe's wife. *(He puts on his gloves.)* Isn't that true? Wouldn't both our minds be full of memories of all the years the four of us were together?

HERMAN.    Goodbye, Christine. Good luck in Florida, and please give my warm regards to Beverly. *(He ascends to entry hall. Christine runs past him, blocks his path to door.)*

CHRISTINE.    I won't let you leave like this.

HERMAN.    Like what?

CHRISTINE.    Hurt, and angry.

HERMAN.    I'm not either one. The only way I'm leaving is with my few remaining shreds of human dignity. *(He tries to move past her galoshes flapping, but she thwarts him.)*

CHRISTINE.    Herman, can't you see? You and I can't even agree on how you're leaving an apartment. We could never agree on anything. From the day we met we were always needling each other. Most of the time it was only *playful* needling, but if we were married we wouldn't use needles, we'd use knives, and we'd play for blood.

HERMAN.    *(Archly.)* Perhaps. Now, in whatever fashion, may I leave? *(She steps aside. Believing he's un-bolting the door, he bolts it, tries to open it, can't. Christine unbolts door, opens it. Herman exits, closing door. Christine walks toward kitchen, as door chimes sound. She comes back, opens door, in comes Herman.)*

CHRISTINE.    Hi there. Long time no see.

HERMAN.    I can't let you do this to yourself.

CHRISTINE.    Do what?

HERMAN.    Make a snap decision which you may later regret. You owe it to your future peace-of-mind to mull it over.

CHRISTINE.    How long?

HERMAN.    *(Checking his wristwatch.)* Three hours. Then I'll pick you up, take you out to dinner, and whatever your non-snap decision is I promise to accept it.

CHRISTINE.    Herman, I can't go out on my last night in town.

HERMAN.    Christine, please. Just a fast bite. One fast bite in honor of more than thirty years of friendship.

CHRISTINE.    *(After a pause, grimly.)* Okay. It's a date. I'd be delighted.

HERMAN.    Well, I better not overstay my welcome. *(He exits, closing door. As Christine starts to bolt it, chimes sound. She opens door, revealing Herman.)* I just thought of another item for my list. Number five: The religious factor. *(A generous "concession.")* If we have children, you can raise them Catholic. *(He exits, closing door.)*

### BLACKOUT

## Scene 2

*Time:   Thursday, early evening.*

*As lights come up:  Diet Pepsi bottle, drinking glasses, and carpet swatches are gone. In the entry hall, nearer to kitchen wing are several sealed Mayflower cartons, and nearer to bedroom wing are two sealed Mayflower wardrobe cartons. At the bookcases are Chuck and Ralph, almost finished packing the items on shelves at their usual work  pace:  Ralph swiftly, Chuck dawdling.*

CHUCK.    Ralph, you know what I been wondering?
RALPH.    Yes. You wonder how you can talk less and work more.
CHUCK.    Something else I wonder is how come there's no *Mister* what's-his-name? Did they get divorced, or did he conk out?
RALPH.    Mr. what's-his-name, otherwise known as Mr. Millman, passed away. One year ago from yesterday.
CHUCK.    How did you find that out?
RALPH.    Good movers always get acquainted with their clients. Not *too* acquainted, just enough to prove we see them as more than our employers, we see them as human beings. *(From bedroom wing comes Christine, wearing slippers and a full-length dressing gown.)*
CHRISTINE.    Fellas, I hate to do this to you, but I have to get something from a wardrobe carton.
CHUCK.    Too late. The wardrobe cartons are already sealed.

24

*(Ralph ascends to entry hall.)*

RALPH.    Mrs. Millman, it's not too late. We're always available for any service you can possibly ask us to perform. *(He proceeds to unseal a carton.)*

CHRISTINE.    I need a dress. For this dinner date I can't get out of. He was too persistent.

RALPH.    *(Waxing gallant.)* And who could blame him?

CHRISTINE.    Thanks, Ralph, but if you're that nearsighted I hope Chuck packed all the glassware. *(Carton unsealed, Ralph opens its flap, then inquires.)*

RALPH.    Would you like me to open the other one too?

CHRISTINE.    First let's see how I do in this one. *(Ralph descends to living room and resumes packing, as Christine sifts through contents of carton.)*

CHUCK.    Ralph, are we gonna take a dinner break?

RALPH.    I haven't decided yet. *(Christine removes a dress that's on a hanger, as Chuck asks Ralph.)*

CHUCK.    When will you decide?

RALPH.    When I reach my decision.

CHRISTINE.    *(Re: dress.)* This'll be fine. You can seal the carton. Tomorrow I'll pack it in my suitcase. *(She exits to bedroom wing.)*

RALPH.    Chuck.

CHUCK.    What?

RALPH.    Go seal the carton.

CHUCK.    Why don't *you* seal it? I sealed it the first time.

RALPH.    And since you did such a good job, do it again. *(Chuck ascends to entry hall, seals carton, during.)*

CHUCK.    Ralph, I'd like you to tell me, I'd really like you to tell me, what gives you the right to be so bossy with me?

RALPH.    Oh, I don't know…. Maybe because I've been with the Mayflower Worldwide Moving Company twenty-six years, and you've been with it three weeks. *(Christine returns, carrying hanger with dress.)*

CHRISTINE.    I tried it on, but it didn't work. Too summery.

CHUCK.    You can wear a heavy sweater.

RALPH.    Chuck, don't be a fashion expert. Just open the other carton. *(Chuck unseals other carton, during:)*

25

CHRISTINE.    Ralph, I want you and Chuck to take a dinner break. I'd make something for you here, but I have no food, so please go out for a nice dinner, and I'll pay for it.

RALPH.    That's very kind of you, but we wouldn't hear of it. We'll just go get take-out sandwiches, so we can finish up without charging you any overtime. *(Carton unsealed, Chuck opens flap. Christine sifts through more clothing. Chuck faces Ralph.)*

CHUCK.    Why sandwiches? Let's get a couple of pizzas. *(Christine removes another dress on a hanger.)*

CHRISTINE.    This'll do it. I'm positive. *(Extending dress #1 to Chuck.)* You can put this back and seal the carton. *(Chuck proceeds to do so.)* I apologize for the inconvenience.

CHUCK.    That's okay, Mrs. ... *(After failing to recall her name.)* That's okay. *(Except for the one CD, the dish of candy, and bottles and glasses on the bar, all items to be packed are now packed. Ralph crosses to bar.)*

CHRISTINE.    Ralph, don't pack the bar. I'll do that later, in case I have to offer my date a quick, quick, quick, quick nightcap. *(She exits to bedroom wing. Chuck descends to living room.)*

RALPH.    Now we'll put cartons in the hallway, so *Mrs. Millman* has more room for entertaining. *(Movers begin taking all cartons to entry hall.)*

CHUCK.    Why didn't you let her buy us dinner? And why shouldn't we go into overtime? Don't we need money more than she does?

RALPH.    Chuck, I'm not a doctor, I'm not a lawyer, I'm a mover.

CHUCK.    What's that got to do with it?

RALPH.    I never take advantage of people who put their trust in me.

CHUCK.    Ralph, I'm hungry. When can we take our dinner break?

RALPH.    Soon.

CHUCK.    How soon?

RALPH.    Soon enough. *(Beat.)* Chuck, I want to tell you something.

CHUCK.    You always do.

RALPH.    I want to tell you that if sometimes I seem a little tough on you, I only do it in the hope I can turn you into a top-flight moving man.

CHUCK.   I don't think I'll ever make it. I don't even think I want to. There's gotta be more to life than packing cartons and lifting furniture.

RALPH.   There is. There's the pride of a job well done.

CHUCK.   I don't want that either. What I want is great-looking clothes, a great-looking sports car, and great-looking women.

RALPH.   How do you plan to get them?

CHUCK.   I'd like to just wake up one morning and there they are.

RALPH.   Chuck, that's the American Dream. And in the words of Abraham Lincoln, it's very stupid.

## BLACKOUT

## Scene 3

*Time:   Thursday night.*

*As lights come up:   The only lights on are in entry hall, which now contains all cartons that were here before, plus more from other areas of the apartment. Front door opens ... Christine enters ... followed by Herman. Over a dress — not the one she selected earlier — she wears a mink coat. Over a handsome suit with shirt and necktie, he wears a dressy overcoat, topped by a homburg. As he closes door and bolts it, she puts her purse and keys on entry hall table, then flicks the switch that turns on living room light. Herman sets his hat on a nearby carton, removes his overcoat. Christine takes it from him, hangs it in guest closet, during:*

HERMAN.   I see you keep your keys on a key ring.

CHRISTINE.   Yes, I do.

HERMAN.   So do I.

CHRISTINE.    At last we have something in common. *(She faces him, marvels.)* I can't get over how spiffy you look.

HERMAN.    To escort a perfect lady one must be a perfect gentleman. *(Turning her back, Christine opens her coat, lets it slide from her shoulders, expecting Herman to help her. But he turns, descends to living room, mink thus falling to floor. She reacts, retrieves mink, hangs it up, as Herman lights the gas fireplace.)* I thought you'd enjoy a last look at your majestic New York fireplace.

CHRISTINE.    Would you like some brandy, or sherry, or a spot of Diet Pepsi? *(She descends to living room.)*

HERMAN.    When did you get Diet Pepsi?

CHRISTINE.    *(Descending to living room.)* I asked my movers to get it when they went out for sandwiches, and I'm glad to see they're gone so they can go to bed early because tomorrow's a very busy day for them.

HERMAN.    Why?

CHRISTINE.    They're loading a truck and driving to Florida.

HERMAN.    I mean why did you ask them to get Diet Pepsi?

CHRISTINE.    To express my appreciation for being invited to the restaurant you called "La Raisinette," which I translated into "La Raison D'Etre."

HERMAN.    You told me, but I forgot — what is that in English?

CHRISTINE.    The reason for existence.

HERMAN.    In their case that's stealing money.

CHRISTINE.    I warned you. I said I heard it was expensive. But you said, and I quote, "Christine, don't bother me with trivia."

HERMAN.    I know, I know; don't rub it in.

CHRISTINE.    How expensive *was* it?

HERMAN.    You'll be happier remaining ignorant.

CHRISTINE.    You shouldn't have let the captain order for us. I bet he picked whatever items cost the most.

HERMAN.    I only did that because you said you had to get home as fast as possible. Besides, I didn't let him order everything; I made him give us our choice of desserts.

CHRISTINE.    Herman, it's late. So please tell me do you or don't you want a very quick nightcap?

HERMAN.   I'd like a glass of sherry — which at La Raise La Prices would undoubtedly cost ten bucks.

CHRISTINE.   *(Crossing to bar.)*   May I offer to pay half of whatever the check was?

HERMAN.   You may offer, but I refuse. It's not your fault. I blame only the person who told me it was a delightful adventure in dining.

CHRISTINE.   Who was that?

HERMAN.   My accountant. Who, if he can afford to eat there, I now suspect of embezzlement.

CHRISTINE.   *(Looking at sherry bottles.)* Do you want dry sherry, or sweet?

HERMAN.   Either one. It doesn't matter. I have no preference.

CHRISTINE.   Then I'll give you dry. There's only a little bit left, and that way I won't have to pack the bottle. *(She pours dry sherry into a cordial glass, emptying the bottle.)* I feel terrible. As I said, I knew it wasn't cheap, but I had no idea it was outrageous.

HERMAN.   I believe you. Otherwise I'm sure that for dessert you never would've ordered fresh raspberries. In February. *(Christine approaches him with the glass of sherry.)* Is it too late to ask for sweet?

CHRISTINE.   If you wanted sweet, why did you — *(Stopping herself, opting not to make an issue of it.)* No, it's not too late. I'll drink the dry. *(She returns to bar, sets down glass, fills another with sweet sherry.)*

HERMAN.   Did you happen to hear tomorrow's weather forecast?

CHRISTINE.   No. I was too busy packing. And I'm still not finished. As soon as you leave I have to do my suitcase and my cosmetics case.

HERMAN.   Snow. All day, and all night. Including at Kennedy Airport. *(Christine crosses with both sherries, gives him the sweet.)*

CHRISTINE.   That doesn't worry me.

HERMAN.   It doesn't? Since when?

CHRISTINE.   I'm never afraid of flying in the snow. I'm only afraid of flying in an airplane. *(She sits on far end of sofa, lifts her glass, proposes a toast.)* Here's to freedom, justice, and peace throughout the world.

HERMAN. *(Lifting his glass.)* And what's more important, here's to *us*.

CHRISTINE. *(Warily.)* In what connection?

HERMAN. May we see each other again. Someday, somewhere, somehow.

CHRISTINE. I'll be back in April, for Billy's bar mitzvah.

HERMAN. Billy who?

CHRISTINE. Billy Stone. My grandson. Last year we put Herman Lewis carpeting in his bedroom.

HERMAN. Oh, *that* Billy. Do you think Joan and Larry will invite me?

CHRISTINE. No, but I think Barbara and Paul will, since they happen to be Billy's parents.

HERMAN. Is it in the beginning of April or the end of April?

CHRISTINE. It's in the middle. April sixteenth.

HERMAN. Today is February fifth. That'll mean more than two months without you. I hope I can survive.

CHRISTINE. You can. Before today you survived since January, and before January you survived since November.

HERMAN. Christine, I'm probably being oversensitive, but by any chance are you accusing me of neglecting you?

CHRISTINE. No. However, it *is* true that when I first became a widow you were very attentive to me ... but then, as time rolled by, you became very *in*attentive. That's perfectly natural, and in no way do I criticize you. Even though, if Moe and Miriam were alive, and *you* were dead, Moe would see your widow at least once a week, like clockwork.

HERMAN. Christine.

CHRISTINE. What?

HERMAN. Are you sure you're not Jewish? *(Beat.)* You overlook the fact that Moe was a furrier. He'd have more time to see my widow. A furrier's pace is much more leisurely.

CHRISTINE. *(Sardonically.)* I wish Moe knew that before he leisurely dropped dead. *(Herman sips sherry, then.)*

HERMAN.   Good sherry. Sweet but not *too* sweet. Just like my hostess.

CHRISTINE.   Thank you — if you meant that as a compliment.

HERMAN.   I did. Experience has taught me that a woman who's too sweet is usually covering up a killer instinct. On the other hand, for *my* taste buds, a woman can never be too spicy. *(Rising.)* And to pay another compliment, you are as spicy as they come. *(He sits down again, close enough to imply.)*

CHRISTINE.   Herman, are you planning to make physical advances?

HERMAN.   If I am, how would they be received?

CHRISTINE.   The same way you'd receive a snake bite on the big guy. *(She moves to far end of sofa. For several moments, awkward silence, broken by.)*

HERMAN.   Dinner cost one hundred and seventy-eight dollars.

CHRISTINE.   You're kidding.

HERMAN.   One hundred and twenty dollars for the meal, plus tax, plus forty-five dollars for lavish tips.

CHRISTINE.   I can't believe it.

HERMAN.   Starting from the top ... One bottle of wine: twenty-nine dollars. Probable retail value, eleven. Salad Mayzone for two: eighteen dollars. Roast rack of lamb for two: fifty-five dollars. Coffee for two: six dollars. And for the crowning glory ... fresh raspberries ... in February ... for one ... twelve dollars.

CHRISTINE.   I'm sorry you let me pry that out of you. *(Coaxingly.)* Herman, please, Let me pay for half.

HERMAN.   No.

CHRISTINE.   Then at least let me pay for the raspberries.

HERMAN.   No. *(After sipping sherry.)* The tips consisted of: thirty dollars for the waiter, five for the busboy, and ten for the captain, who miraculously appeared when you were on your final raspberry to ask me: "Masieur, is everysing satisfactory?" And he asked it as if I said no he'd slash his wrists.

CHRISTINE.   So why did you tip him ten dollars?

HERMAN.   If he got any less he'd make the coat check girl impound your mink. That reminds me; I tipped *her* two dollars — so my previous figure was low, and the correct grand total was one hundred and eighty dollars. *(He drains his glass.)*

CHRISTINE.   More sherry?

HERMAN.   That depends on whether you want me to stay here or go home.

CHRISTINE.   Let's compromise. Have another *half* a glass of sherry — then go home. *(She rises, extends her hand for his glass. He doesn't give it to her.)*

HERMAN.   Christine, please don't stand on ceremony. If tonight isn't turning out the way you thought it would, just say so, and I'll leave.

CHRISTINE.   Stay. I insist. Tonight is turning out the way I thought it would. *(She takes his glass, meticulously fills it halfway with sherry.)*

HERMAN.   I'm glad to hear that. I was afraid I can't compete with all the other men whose hearts you're breaking by deserting them. With your charm and beauty I bet there are hundreds of them.

CHRISTINE.   Wrong. My dates are few and far between. And I never get the cream of the crop. The cream of the crop — meaning those who can leave the house without their doctors' permission — all look for women young enough to be their granddaughters. *(Bringing glass to him.)* And they find them, and nobody disapproves, nobody even bats an eye. *(Herman reaches for glass. Christine doesn't notice.)* In contrast, if a *woman* in her sixties dates a man in his thirties, or forties, or even fifties, everybody's shocked. Everybody thinks she's keeping him, and she's nothing but an old, foolish, desperate sugar mommy. *(She gives him glass, sits on sofa.)*

HERMAN.   Reading between the lines, I gather it's conceivable that the right man could keep you in New York.

CHRISTINE.   My right man died a year ago. And there's no man anywhere who can give me what I lost.

HERMAN.   Don't you think that's sort of a defeatist attitude?

CHRISTINE.   How often do *you* go on dates?

HERMAN.   For reasons other than sex?

CHRISTINE.   I withdraw the question.

HERMAN.   Why? Is sex something to hide, like carpet

samples?

CHRISTINE.    There's a vast difference between hiding and bragging.

HERMAN.    Bragging? In what way am I bragging?

CHRISTINE.    You want to make it crystal clear that even though you're a senior citizen you're still as frisky as a colt.

HERMAN.    I deny that. When I brag I say frisky as a stallion.

CHRISTINE.    Well, whatever kind of horse you are, if you're whinnying in my direction, just think of me as the old gray mare.

HERMAN.    You never have sex? Or you ain't what you used to be?

CHRISTINE.    Shall we finish our sherry? *(They sip. Silence, until.)*

HERMAN.    So it looks like you're moving to Florida.

CHRISTINE.    Oh, good, you remembered! Herman, I don't care what people say;  your mind is still sharp as a tack.

HERMAN.    And there's nothing I can do to make you reconsider.

CHRISTINE.    That's correct. *(He moves one cushion closer to her, sniffs the air.)*

HERMAN.    Tell me about the perfume you're wearing.

CHRISTINE.    What would you like to know?

HERMAN.    Why is it giving me the strange sensation that my entire body is on fire?

CHRISTINE.    You're probably having an attack of shingles. *(She rises, crosses to the armchair, sits, sips sherry, then makes casual conversation.)* What's new with your son?

HERMAN.    Steven?

CHRISTINE.    Do you have another one?

HERMAN.    He's fine. *(He sips sherry.)*

CHRISTINE.    How much is left?

HERMAN.    *(Inspecting glass.)* Half the half. Which since these are my last moments with you until April, I plan to slowly savor to its fullest.

CHRISTINE.    How often do you talk to him?

HERMAN.    How often do I talk to who?

CHRISTINE.    Steven.

HERMAN.    Oh. I talk to him, in round numbers, once a

month.

CHRISTINE.    You talk to your only child only once a month? That doesn't sound very ... devoted father and son.

HERMAN.    I live on the east coast, he lives on the west coast; we're devoted from coast to coast.

CHRISTINE.    When's the last time you saw each other? *(Receiving no reply.)* Wasn't it three years ago, at Miriam's funeral?

HERMAN.    If you knew, why did you ask?

CHRISTINE.    To encourage you to get off your behind, get on an airplane, and get some pleasure from your child and your grandchildren.

HERMAN.    Maybe I will. This August there's a carpet convention in Los Angeles, and I'm considering attending.

CHRISTINE.    Herman, don't consider it — *do* it. Not just for your sake, for theirs. Especially Josh and Jenny. They're forgetting what a great guy their grandpa is.

HERMAN.    Not great enough. Otherwise I'd be engaged to be married. *(He sips sherry.)*

CHRISTINE.    How much is left now?

HERMAN.    *(Inspecting glass.)* Half the half the half. I'd be engaged to the woman who even when she sits far away from me, her aroma stirs me to the heights of wanting to swoop her in my arms and smother her with kisses. *(She sets down her glass, rises.)*

CHRISTINE.    So it looks like I'm moving to Florida. If I ever finish packing.

HERMAN.    Well, let it never be said that I can't take a hint. *(He drains his glass, sets it down, rises, crosses to her.)* Goodnight, Christine. Goodnight, and good-bye. *(He takes both her hands.)*

CHRISTINE.    I'll call you in a few days. It's important to me that we keep in touch. *(She tries to free her hands.)*

HERMAN.    Don't go! Stay here and marry me!

CHRISTINE.    *(Tugging her hands free.)* Herman, please. Give up. *(He kneels on one knee, and spreads his arms.)*

HERMAN.    Christine, marry me! A proud man sinks to his knees to beg!

CHRISTINE.    You only sank to one knee. *(He kneels on both knees.)* I loved that movie.

HERMAN.   What movie?

CHRISTINE.   *Moulin Rouge.* The story of Toulouse-Lautrec.

HERMAN.   *(Getting to his feet.)* Mrs. Millman, thank you for a lovely evening, and for one hundred and eighty dollars' worth of mental agony. *(He strides to entry hall. Christine chases him, grabs his elbow.)*

CHRISTINE.   Herman, wait! I'm sorry. I apologize.

HERMAN.   Too late. There's a point where even I can be humiliated.

CHRISTINE.   Forgive me. I'll make it up to you.

HERMAN.   *(Willing to negotiate.)* How?

CHRISTINE.   I'll give you all the sherry you can drink. *(She escorts him to the sofa, he sits. She gets his glass, fills it at bar.)* I really am sorry, but I didn't know how else to handle it. I couldn't marry *anyone* on such short notice. I'm cautious. *(Crossing with sherry.)* Before Moe and I got married, we went steady for three years. *(She hands him the glass, sits beside him.)*

HERMAN.   I'm impetuous. Miriam and I got married after only two short but grueling months.

CHRISTINE.   Grueling for you, or grueling for her?

HERMAN.   For both of us. I assume she told you she was a virgin until her wedding night.

CHRISTINE.   She did. But in those days that was socially acceptable.

HERMAN.   *(After sipping sherry.)* Were you a virgin until your wedding night?

CHRISTINE.   What did Moe tell you?

HERMAN.   Nothing. He always ducked the question.

CHRISTINE.   Well, I won't. *(Touching all bases.)* What did Miriam tell you?

HERMAN.   She also ducked the question.

CHRISTINE.   Yes. I was a virgin until my wedding night.

HERMAN.   Even though you and Moe went steady for three years?

CHRISTINE.   If you think I'm lying — prove it.

HERMAN.   *(Realizing he can't.)* Why are we discussing ancient history? My motto is: Live for today. *(He sets down his glass, then swiftly leans over and kisses Christine on the mouth. Just as*

*swiftly, she pulls away, indignantly slaps his arm.)*
CHRISTINE. Herman, how dare you! *(She springs to her feet and stalks to the entry hall. Herman rises, calls.)*
HERMAN. Christine, don't leave! This is your apartment.
CHRISTINE. *(Crossing to hall table.)* I'm paying for my dinner.
HERMAN. *(Hurrying up to her.)* Christine, I'm sorry. I lost my self control. *(From her purse she takes a checkbook and a pen, starts writing a check.)*
CHRISTINE. Half of one hundred and eighty is ninety.
HERMAN. Christine, please. I profoundly apologize.
CHRISTINE. But you didn't have dessert, and you claim my raspberries cost twelve dollars ... so I owe you one hundred and two dollars.
HERMAN. I accepted *your* apology — why won't you accept mine? *(She tears check from book, extends it to him.)*
CHRISTINE. Here. Take it.
HERMAN. I refuse. *(He backs away, she advances.)* Christine, you already slapped me once; don't slap me twice. *(As she keeps stalking him.)* Would Miriam behave this way with Moe, if they were down here and we were up there? Would she go to this extreme if he drank half a bottle of wine and nearly two glasses of sherry and kissed *her?*
CHRISTINE. How fascinating. When you think it can get you off the hook, up there suddenly exists.
HERMAN. I'm not an atheist — I'm only an agnostic.
CHRISTINE. You're also, for a man your age, excessively horny.
HERMAN. I know. It's like a sickness with me. *(Crossing to her.)* But with your help I think I can be cured. *(Snatching check.)* Besides, you did it wrong. First you subtract the twelve, divide by two, then add back the twelve. *(He tears up check. They descend to living room. He sits on sofa.)* When did *Moe* first kiss you? I just thought I'd compare notes.
CHRISTINE. *(Hoping to shame him.)* Moe first kissed me on our seventh date.
HERMAN. Why was he so bashful? In those days weren't all models rumored to be pushovers?
CHRISTINE. Not fur models. Maybe carpet models, but not

36

fur models.

HERMAN. Where did the kiss occur?

CHRISTINE. *(Fondly recalling.)* In a night club. Lou Walter's Latin Quarter. I don't know why he picked it, because they had a band that specialized in rumbas, sambas, and mambos ... and all Moe could do, and badly, was one basic fox-trot step. But he asked me — I remember as if it was yesterday — "Miss Twinkletoes, would you care to trip the light fantastic?" In those days I was Little Miss Twinkletoes at every dance there was ... so we danced. And whatever music they played, Moe led me in his only step, like a farmer pushing a plow, while he said the band had no rhythm, or the floor was too crowded, or anything except he couldn't dance. But he tried, and he kept trying for the next thirty-eight years, with almost no improvement. I didn't care. I knew, that night, in Lou Walter's Latin Quarter, I found a man who was so sweet ... so dear ... so special ... I wanted to spend the rest of my life with him. *(She sits in armchair.)*

HERMAN. I kissed Miriam on our second date. It was her limited way of thanking me for taking her to a concert at Carnegie Hall, featuring, as I recall, a nineteen-hour flute solo.

CHRISTINE. I only heard about your first date. At Coney Island. When she refused to ride in the Tunnel of Love.

HERMAN. That's why our second date was to prove I was a man of great refinement. I didn't fool her, but from that moment on she had a terrific excuse to throw me into a bottomless pit of: Operas. Ballets. Museums. Art galleries. Lectures. Foreign movies filmed in total darkness. The Experimental Theatre of the Living Dead. The Flying Folk Dancers of Tasmania. You name it, in my wife's lifelong and relentless search for culture, I saw it.

CHRISTINE. Herman, level with me. Do you have any *happy* memories of Miriam?

HERMAN. Yes. But it depresses me to dwell on them. *(He sips sherry. She rises. He shows her his glass.)* There's still some left.

CHRISTINE. *(Crossing to built-in stereo.)* I'm not kicking you out. I just want to show you what I listened to while I was waiting for you to pick me up. *(She takes the open case of the CD*

*Chuck left for her, reads its title.)* "A Stereo Stroll Down Memory Lane. 50 Instrumental Favorites From Way Back When." Would you like to hear a few of them, before you leave?

HERMAN.   Fine. In that case I don't have to nurse my sherry. *(He finishes it, sets down glass. She puts down CD case, turns on the stereo. Over its loudspeakers comes "Sentimental Journey."\*)*

CHRISTINE.   *(Facing Herman.)* Contestant number one, can you name that tune?

HERMAN.   "Sentimental Journey." *(She resumes her seat. They listen, then he sings.)* Seven, that's the time I leave, at seven ... I'll be waitin' up for heaven ...

CHRISTINE.   *(Singing.)* Countin' every mile of railroad track that takes me back ...

HERMAN.   Never knew my heart could be so yearny ...

CHRISTINE.   Why did I decide to roam?

HERMAN and CHRISTINE.   *(In unison.)* Gonna take a sentimental journey ... sentimental journey home. *(The music ends.)*

HERMAN.   You know what that song has that songs of to-day *don't* have?

CHRISTINE.   Yes. A melody. *(Next song plays. "Besame Mucho,"\*\* a rumba. Herman identifies it.)*

HERMAN.   "Besame mucho."

CHRISTINE.   Do you know the words?

HERMAN.   No.

CHRISTINE.   Good. *(As she sways to the music. He rises, crosses to her.)*

HERMAN.   Miss Twinkletoes, would you care to trip the light fantastic?

CHRISTINE.   Can you still rumba?

HERMAN.   Can birds still fly? *(Christine rises ... and they dance, at arm's length ... at first tentatively, but soon smoothly, gaining confidence. He "casually" leads her to entry hall, then off-stage toward bedroom wing. They quickly return, Christine pushing him. Song ends, next one plays. It's "In the Mood,"\*\* a sprightly Lindy. Herman and*

* See Special Note on Music on copyright page.
** See Special Note on Songs and Recordings on copyright page.

*Christine jitterbug, exuberantly, like two kids at a High School prom. Song ends, dancers separate.)*
CHRISTINE.   Thank you. That was fun.
HERMAN.   Then let's keep going. *(Next song plays. "I'm In the Mood For Love,"\*\* a dreamy fox-trot.)*
CHRISTINE.   Are you a glutton for punishment?
HERMAN.   Only with my accountant. *(They dance, at arm's length. Spins, breaks, deep dips, the works. They dance closer, until they're cheek to cheek ... then they kiss ... and keep kissing until song ends and next one plays. It's the bouncy "Pennsylvania Polka"\*\* — and it causes Christine to end the kiss, run to the stereo, and turn it off. Herman runs to her, again takes her in his arms, kisses her. She responds, then pulls away.)*
CHRISTINE.   Herman, go home. Go home instantly.
HERMAN.   I hear you with my ears — but not with my lips. *(He takes her in his arms.)*
CHRISTINE.   Herman, we can't do this!
HERMAN.   We're two mature people. As a matter of fact, between us we're a hundred and twenty-six years old. *(He kisses her, then.)*
CHRISTINE.   I'm a Catholic grandmother! I don't put out on the first date!
HERMAN.   Christine, I say this to you in all sincerity. Let's go to bed. *(He kisses her face and neck.)*
CHRISTINE.   I don't have time. I have to pack my suitcase and my cosmetics case and my suitcase and — okay! Yes! Let's go to bed! *(He runs to entry hall. She calls.)* Herman.
HERMAN.   What?
CHRISTINE.   Wait for me! *(She joins him, grabs his hand, and they run off-stage to bedroom wing.)*

## THE CURTAIN FALLS

\*\* See Special Note on Songs and Recordings on copyright page.

# ACT TWO

*Time: Friday morning.*

*At rise: Front door open, all moving cartons gone, bookcases and coffee table barren, but all furniture and pictures in place. Ralph and Chuck enter from bedroom wing, carrying king-sized box springs which they lean against wall alongside door.*

CHUCK. What's our game plan for the drive? Are we gonna drive straight through, or are we gonna stop a lot to eat and sleep?

RALPH. We'll see how we feel as we go along.

CHUCK. If we drive straight through we can spend a day on the beach before we have to drive back. You like the beach, don't you?

RALPH. Only if it's near the water. *(Dressed for traveling, Christine enters from kitchen wing.)*

CHRISTINE. I just put up some coffee.

CHUCK. Ralph, it's time for a coffee break.

RALPH. Not yet. When the coffee is ready is when it's time for a coffee break. So meanwhile go get the headboard. *(Chuck exits to bedroom wing.)* Mrs. Millman, are you okay?

CHRISTINE. I'm fine.

RALPH. Good. Because to me you seem sort of ... I don't know ... part tired part nervous.

CHRISTINE. I am. I'm nervous about moving, I'm tired from being out for dinner much later than I expected. *(Chuck returns, with a headboard. He leans against boxed springs.)*

RALPH. But the nervous part is normal. All clients get nervous on moving day. Especially if they lived in their homes as long as you did. Every item they see carried out tells a tale of the story of their life. *(Movers exit to bedroom wing, as the intercom buzzes. Christine crosses, flicks switch, converses with doorman in lobby.)*

CHRISTINE.   Yes?... Special delivery of what?... Why can't *you* sign for it?... Oh, all right, I don't understand, but send him up. *(She turns off intercom. Movers enter carrying a mattress. They lean it against springs, during:)*

RALPH.   Mrs. Millman, in terms of furniture telling stories, I once had a client who saw me taking out her mattress, and she said to me "Oh boy, if that mattress could only talk!"

CHUCK.   And you probably said "It's time for a coffee break."

RALPH.   That's right. But then I added "After we get the bed frame." *(Movers exit to bedroom wing, while Christine descends to living room, sits on sofa. In the front doorway appears Herman, in same overcoat, hat, muffler, and gloves he wore at top of Act One. Behind his back he conceals a large gift-wrapped box. He knocks on door. Startled, Christine whirls, sees him.)*

HERMAN.   *(Cheerfully.)* Good morning. Special delivery. I hid my true identity on the outside chance you left orders with the doorman not to let me in.

CHRISTINE.   That never occurred to me. Why would I think anyone would just pop in on me on my last and hectic day in town?

HERMAN.   *(Descending to living room.)* You don't look hectic. You look like you're calmly sitting and wondering if leaving town is what you really want to do.

CHRISTINE.   I'm hectic. If I don't look hectic it's only because I've been hectic since the crack of dawn, and this was my first chance to sit down and take a break from being hectic.

HERMAN.   Technically I *am* a delivery man. I'm delivering *(Displaying gift box.)* five pounds of assorted chocolates. You can eat them on the plane, to distract you from your morbid fear of going down in flames. *(He gives her the box. She puts it on coffee table.)* I also popped in so we can talk things over.

CHRISTINE.   Talk *what* things over?

HERMAN.   The events that transpired last night.

CHRISTINE.   Herman, how can you be so insensitive? Don't you know I'm embarrassed to see you so soon after we

41

allowed ourselves to make a terrible mistake.

HERMAN. Christine, even if what was done was a mistake — and I'm far from ready to admit it was — there's still no reason not to talk about it, and try to *learn* from our mistake.

CHRISTINE. I already learned. I'll never dance with you again. *(Unseen by those in living room, Ralph and Chuck enter, carrying a metal bed frame.)*

HERMAN. I suppose I should conclude from that that you'll also never go to bed with me again.

RALPH. *(Calling.)* Mrs. Millman.

CHRISTINE. *(Whirling, realizing movers overheard what Herman just said.)* Oh my God!

HERMAN. *(To Ralph and Chuck.)* Who're you?

RALPH. We're the movers. Who're you?

HERMAN. I'm Herman Lewis. Mrs. Millman's cherished friend of more than thirty years. *(Christine rises, faces entry hall, as movers prop frame against mattress.)*

CHRISTINE. Ralph, Chuck … in case you overheard what Mr. Lewis just said to me … it was the punch line of a joke.

CHUCK. You didn't laugh.

CHRISTINE. It wasn't funny.

RALPH. Chuck, we'll put the bed stuff in the truck, then we'll take our coffee break.

CHUCK. Unless you find another excuse to postpone it. *(Movers pick up the bed frame and the mattress, carry them out front door. Christine faces Herman.)*

CHRISTINE. Well, are you satisfied?

HERMAN. Am I satisfied by what?

CHRISTINE. You made me feel dirt cheap in front of my moving men. *(Herman removes one glove.)* Herman, don't undress. *(Movers return, pick up headboard and box springs, exit front door.)*

HERMAN. Christine, talk to me for five minutes. Just five minutes.

CHRISTINE. Herman, please don't think I'm being hostile. I still hold warm affection for you. As soon as I'm settled in Florida I'll send you a nice long newsy postcard.

HERMAN. Just five minutes. Just five minutes. *(Picking up*

*candy box.)* That's one minute per pound. *(Christine sighs, sits in armchair. Herman takes off other glove, hat, muffler, and overcoat, under which he's dressed for a day at work. He sets all his garments on the ottoman, then sits on sofa. Christine checks her wristwatch.)*

CHRISTINE.   It's nine forty-five. You've got until nine-fifty.

HERMAN.   Don't start timing before I give you somebody's love.

CHRISTINE.   Whose?

HERMAN.   My son's. I talked to him this morning. He said "Give my love to Aunt Christine."

CHRISTINE.   *(Apprehensively.)* Did he call you or did you call him?

HERMAN.   I called him. Bright and early, so I could catch him before he went onto his tennis court. And I did. I forgot the time zones. In California it was five A.M.

CHRISTINE.   I hope, and I trust, you didn't tell him about last night.

HERMAN.   What for? He wouldn't be impressed. He probably spends a hundred and eighty dollars for dinner seven nights a week.

CHRISTINE.   That's not what I meant, and you know it.

HERMAN.   I didn't tell him. I don't plan to tell anybody. Not even my accountant, and he tries to make me tell him *everything.*

CHRISTINE.   *(Checking wristwatch.)* Nine forty-six. You've got until nine fifty-one.

HERMAN.   Then without further ado, now that you slept on it, what's your considered opinion of our first mutual sexual experience?

CHRISTINE.   Herman, are you really going to force me to discuss this?

HERMAN.   Yes — and add ten seconds for asking a question that you already knew the answer to.

CHRISTINE.   How blunt can I be? As opposed to how tactful must I be?

HERMAN.   Christine, in more than thirty years have you ever known me to care about being tactful?

CHRISTINE.   No, now that you mention it, I haven't.

HERMAN. Then add ten more seconds for another point-less question.

CHRISTINE. Okay. Then being blunt ... I was slightly disappointed.

HERMAN. Why?

CHRISTINE. I guess I expected too much, after all the advance publicity about the big guy. I couldn't wait to meet him. And for a few suspenseful moments I didn't, I only met his cousin, Gentle Ben.

HERMAN. Did anything else fall short of your expectations?

CHRISTINE. I wanted to see if making love could become part of my life again. Without feeling I was betraying my husband, and hating myself, and blaming *you*, and hating you.

HERMAN. You only said you were slightly disappointed; you didn't say you hated it.

CHRISTINE. I didn't. I liked being held, and being kissed, and being close ... and you were tender, and considerate ... and even though I can't claim to be an expert on this, I think your technique was very nice.

HERMAN. Thank you.

CHRISTINE. But that's *all* that last night was. Nice. Not superb, not sensational, not magnificent, not —

HERMAN. *(Interrupting.)* Christine, I get the message. So stop repeating yourself, and just tell me how you rate it on a scale of one to ten, ten being top.

CHRISTINE. *(Upon reflection.)* Four.

HERMAN. *(Taken aback.)* Four?

CHRISTINE. Maybe five. But either way, it was several points below the heights of ecstasy, and if you're still hoping it was enough to change my mind about Florida — forget it.

HERMAN. On a scale of one to ten, I rate it nine.

CHRISTINE. Do you? Do you really rate it nine?

HERMAN. No. I made a stab at being tactful. I really rate it eight. Or seven. Or six. Five.

CHRISTINE. Good. Because I'd know you were lying if you denied that you were nervous, and tense, and anxious, and —

HERMAN. *(Interrupting.)* Christine, you're doing it again.

CHRISTINE. Doing what?

HERMAN. Using nineteen words that say the same thing.

CHRISTINE. I'm sorry. I'll add another ten seconds.

HERMAN. As I view the basic problem ... now that I also had a chance to sleep on it ... *(Their return unnoticed, Ralph and Chuck enter, stand in entry hall.)* The problem wasn't *that* we went to bed together, it was *where* we went to bed together.

RALPH. *(Calling.)* Mrs. Millman. *(She whirls, sees movers, then rises and bursts into laughter.)*

CHRISTINE. *(To Herman.)* Now *that* one was funny! *(She ascends to entry hall, as Herman rises, turns, calls to movers.)*

HERMAN. The next time you guys barge in here, will you kindly knock?

RALPH. *(Defensively.)* We're not barging in — we're working.

HERMAN. Well, knock anyhow.

RALPH. Mrs. Millman, when can we can load the living room?

CHRISTINE. As soon as Mr. Lewis leaves. At approximately ... *(Checking wristwatch.)* Nine fifty-four. Now I'll get your coffee. *(She shoots Herman a look, then walks toward kitchen wing. Herman calls.)*

HERMAN. Christine, I'd appreciate some coffee too. *(She exits. Herman rises, crosses to steps to entry hall, addresses Chuck.)* Ralph. *(To Ralph.)* Chuck.

RALPH. I'm Ralph; he's Chuck.

HERMAN. Excuse me. Ralph, may I ask you and Chuck a question?

RALPH. Shoot.

HERMAN. How would each of you like to earn an extra two hundred bucks apiece?

CHUCK. What do we have to do for it?

HERMAN. Walk off the job. Leave whatever you didn't load unloaded, get in your truck, and drive away.

RALPH. I don't think our client would like that.

HERMAN. Yes she would. She doesn't really want to move to Florida, but she thinks it's too late for her to change her mind.

RALPH. It isn't. All she has to do is tell me. Personally. That means her, not you.

HERMAN.    She's reluctant to admit it, even to herself. Besides, that way you and Chuck won't get the extra bonus.

RALPH.    And what would we tell the Mayflower Worldwide Moving Company?

HERMAN.    Nothing. Have them send me the bill for all cost up to now, and I'll pay it.

RALPH.    Sorry, we can't do that.

HERMAN.    Why not?

RALPH.    A: It's unethical. B: We don't want to lose our jobs.

CHUCK.    *(To Herman.)* Not for just two hundred bucks. *(Christine comes back with a kitchen counter breadboard used as a tray to carry three paper cups with coffee, paper napkins, and two doughnuts.)*

RALPH.    Chuck, carry that for her. *(Chuck takes board, brings it to coffee table, sets it down, Christine following.)*

HERMAN.    *(To Ralph.)* If I was Mr. Mayflower I'd make you stop pushing Chuck around.

RALPH.    If you were Mr. Mayflower, I'd apply for a job with Bekins. *(They descend to living room. Herman sits on sofa. Chuck sets down board, sits next to Herman, to his annoyance. Christine picks up two cups, gives one to each mover.)*

CHRISTINE.    *(The gracious hostess.)* Chuck … Ralph … *(She gets another cup and gives it to Herman, less graciously.)* Here. *(She picks up doughnuts with napkins.)* I found a couple of dough- nuts.

HERMAN.    Are they plain or sugared?

CHRISTINE.    They're glazed, and they're for Ralph and Chuck. *(She gives one to Chuck.)*

RALPH.    None for me. I had a big breakfast.

HERMAN.    I didn't. I had no breakfast whatsoever.

CHRISTINE.    Chuck, maybe you'd like *two.*

RALPH.    He wouldn't. He'd like *you* to have one.

HERMAN.    I didn't have *time* for breakfast. I had to shop for a five-pound box of candy. *(Christine gives doughnut to him. He takes a bite.)*

RALPH.    You could at least offer to split it with her.

CHRISTINE.    *(Jokingly.)* Too many calories. I only eat *choco-*

*late* doughnuts.

CHUCK. *(Appreciatively.)* That's a good one, Mrs. Maxwell.

RALPH. Mrs. Millman, Mrs. Millman. *(To Christine.)* We'll take our break in the kitchen. *(Chuck rises, he and Ralph exit to kitchen wing. Christine sits on sofa.)*

HERMAN. I assume you're going to subtract however long it took for the miscellaneous intrusions.

CHRISTINE. Herman, let's turn off the time clock. Let's just get whatever it is we're doing over with as soon as possible. I'm tired, and I'm busy, and I'm moving.

HERMAN. *(After sipping coffee.)* I believe we left off with my statement that the problem was *where* we went to bed, not *that* we went to bed. *(They both look toward kitchen, to make sure movers didn't return.)*

CHRISTINE. You know where *I* wish we went to bed?

HERMAN. Where?

CHRISTINE. *(Pointing upward.)* Up there. So I'd already *be* there, and I wouldn't have to be afraid that God won't let me in.

HERMAN. Don't worry, God will let you in. If He doesn't, Miriam will noodgy him through all eternity. *(Beat.)* But I agree using the bed you shared with your late husband and my late best friend was a definite strategic error. It made me feel inhibited. It made me feel that Moe was in the room, looking over my shoulder.

CHRISTINE. If Moe was in the room, I'm sure he would've spoken to his widow, unless what he saw her doing gave him another heart attack.

HERMAN. I don't mean I actually saw him, he was only there in spirit, in my mind.

CHRISTINE. Was Miriam, there too, in spirit, in your mind?

HERMAN. No. Her spirit couldn't get away. It was at a concert. *(He eats more doughnut.)* Good doughnut. Where'd you get it?

CHRISTINE. In a doughnut shop.

HERMAN. Therefore, under those circumstances … I say … let's not get discouraged. Let's try again. On neutral territory. In a hotel room. On our honeymoon. *(Pause, then he points to candy box.)* You didn't read the gift card. It's inside. *(She opens box, removes card, but has trouble reading it, until Herman lends her his glasses. As the movers return to entry hall, Christine reads.)*

CHRISTINE.  Roses are red, chocolates are brown. Don't take your body out of town.

RALPH.  Mrs. Millman.

CHRISTINE.  *(Trying to cover.)* He even puts jokes on gift cards. He loves to laugh, even though you'd never guess it from looking at him.

HERMAN.  Christine, don't grovel. They're supposed to knock.

RALPH.  Mrs. Millman, we're ready to load the living room.

CHRISTINE.  Please do.

RALPH.  *(To Chuck.)* Did you bring up the box for the pictures?

CHUCK.  No, I thought you did.

HERMAN.  *(Gloating.)* Aha! Total confusion!

RALPH.  *(Descending to living room.)* Chuck, go get the box. *(Chuck exits. Christine puts candy box on cushion next to her. Ralph gets breadboard, deposits it on Herman's lap, then Ralph picks up the coffee table, carries it to entry hall, exits. Herman sets breadboard on floor. Christine eats a piece of candy.)*

HERMAN.  Is it good?

CHRISTINE.  It's adequate. *(She eats a second piece, as Herman finishes his coffee, wipes his mouth with napkin, crumples it, puts it in cup, puts cup on breadboard, gets back to the subject of sex.)*

HERMAN.  For the first time, a rating of five is nothing to sneeze at. And in the future, if we both apply ourselves, I'm sure we can bring it up to ten. Practice makes perfect. *(This prompts Christine to reach for another chocolate, but she withdraws her hand, rises, carries candy box to bar, telling herself.)*

CHRISTINE.  Maybe if I keep it further away from me. *(She sets box on bar, faces Herman.)* Herman, why all the emphasis on sex? For people in our age group is sex that important?

HERMAN.  Absolutely. It doesn't matter what your age is. As long as your equipment is functioning, sex is the staff of life.

CHRISTINE.  I always thought the staff of life is bread.

HERMAN.  Only if you're starving. Or in the baking business.

CHRISTINE. *(Sitting on sofa.)* What's the age group of your other recent bed partners?

HERMAN. It varies.

CHRISTINE. From what to what? Twenty to ninety? Thirty to eighty? Forty to sixty?

HERMAN. Christine, what's the difference? In all age groups the group is relatively small.

CHRISTINE. You're just being modest. Last night you said you're as frisky as a stallion.

HERMAN. I exaggerated.

CHRISTINE. Why?

HERMAN. I was trying to be as alluring to you as you are to me.

CHRISTINE. I see. Now tell me the truth. In the three years you've been a widower, how many women have you gone to bed with? You can round it off to the nearest hundred.

HERMAN. Two.

CHRISTINE. Two hundred?

HERMAN. No, two women.

CHRISTINE. Including me?

HERMAN. Yes.

CHRISTINE. You were right. That's a relatively small number. *(Beat.)* When did the affair begin? And is it still continuing?

HERMAN. It wasn't an affair. We only did it once. She gave it to me for my birthday.

CHRISTINE. And how did you rate it, on a scale of one to ten?

HERMAN. *(After pondering.)* Eight.

CHRISTINE. Beats my five. Was she younger, and prettier?

HERMAN. Younger, yes. But you're far, far, far, far prettier.

CHRISTINE. Then how come she got a higher rating?

HERMAN. It was psychological. She's my accountant's sister. I was doing to her what her brother so often does to me. *(The movers return with picture box. Ralph knocks on door.)* Thanks, but this time it wasn't necessary. *(Movers descend to living room, as Christine rises, picks up breadboard, informing Herman.)*

CHRISTINE. I'll be right back to say good-bye to you. *(She exits to kitchen wing. Ralph and Chuck proceed to take pictures from walls, put them in box.)*

HERMAN.   Ralph, Chuck ... four.

CHUCK.   Four what?

HERMAN.   I'm upping my offer. If you walk off the job I'll pay you four hundred bucks apiece.

CHUCK.   In cash?

RALPH.   What's the difference? *(To Herman.)* You're wasting your time. We're not even tempted.

HERMAN.   I think Chuck is tempted. *(Christine returns, descends to living room.)*

RALPH.   Mrs. Millman, do all the pictures go to Florida?

CHRISTINE.   No, they all go into storage — except for that one. *(She indicates the abstract oil above mantelpiece.)*

RALPH.   It's very unusual. What's it supposed to be?

CHRISTINE.   I don't know — but it was painted by my daughter Joan.

CHUCK.   How old is she?

CHRISTINE.   Now she's thirty-two, but she did it when she was in high school.

CHUCK.   I figured she did it in kindergarten. *(Everyone else glares at him.)* Isn't it finger-painting?

RALPH.   No. It's contemporary modern art.

CHUCK.   *(To Christine.)* No offense, Mrs. Miller. *(Ralph takes down oil.)*

CHRISTINE.   *(To Chuck.)* You're getting warmer. *(Movers exit.)* Herman, I'm curious. What prompted you to call Steven?

HERMAN.   You did. You said I should tell him I'm coming to L.A. for a carpet convention, so I told him.

CHRISTINE.   And?

HERMAN.   He won't be there. He's taking Josh and Jenny to Hawaii, for the entire month of August.

CHRISTINE.   Can't he take them in July? They're out of school then too.

HERMAN.   I don't know if he can change the reservation.

CHRISTINE.   This far in advance? Did you at least suggest he try?

HERMAN.   No.

CHRISTINE.   Why not?

HERMAN.  I wanted *him* to suggest it.

CHRISTINE.  Maybe August is the only time he can get away from work.

HERMAN.  Then he could've said: "Dad, for a chance to be with *you*, we'll only go for three weeks." Or else he could've said: "Dad, either before or after the convention, why don't you join us in Hawaii?"

CHRISTINE.  You're right, he could have, and he should have. *(Herman rises, goes to windows, looks out. Christine sits on sofa.)*

HERMAN.  I guess it's time for me to face the fact that my son and I don't have a close relationship.

CHRISTINE.  I'm sorry. You did when he was little. What happened?

HERMAN.  He outgrew me. I had to quit high school and go to work. He finished high school, and college, and medical school. Then he moved to California and learned *other* things that I don't know. Where to get a fifty-dollar haircut ... how to talk for twenty minutes about wine ... how to socialize with movie stars ... all the stuff that makes him too classy for a guy whose only stock in trade is peddling rugs.

CHRISTINE.  Are you saying Steven is ashamed of you?

HERMAN.  No. I think he loves me, and I know I love him, and I'm proud of his success — but what it all boils down to is we're just not each other's type. That's why he never confides in me, about his hopes and dreams, or what went wrong with his two marriages, and that's why even though I'll always be his father and he'll always be my son, there's not much chance we can ever be good friends. *(He sits in armchair.)*

CHRISTINE.  Do you feel he was closer to Miriam?

HERMAN.  Definitely. Until ... *(Trails off.)*

CHRISTINE.  Until what?

HERMAN.  There's no point in going into it.

CHRISTINE.  I bet I know what you were going to say.

HERMAN.  Until she was withering away from cancer. For two years. Her only child, who she adored, flew in to visit her three times, and each time he only stayed one day. Miriam never said how much that hurt her, but I think it hurt her more than all her other pains combined. *(Beat.)* Do you win your bet?

CHRISTINE.   Yes, unfortunately I do.

HERMAN.   When I pleaded with him to come more often, and stay longer, he said he couldn't handle it. He couldn't bear to watch her die. A doctor, who works in hospitals and sees death all around him, and never lets it spoil his tennis game. *(Christine rises, crosses, kneels next to him, touches his arm.)*

CHRISTINE.   You're being too hard on him. It doesn't matter what your occupation is — losing someone you love is very difficult to cope with.

HERMAN.   I coped with it. So did you. So did your daughters.

CHRISTINE.   We had it easier. Moe went quickly; we didn't have to see him suffer. If we did, I think Joan and Barbara would've found it just as unbearable as Steven did.

HERMAN.   What about you?

CHRISTINE.   I'm glad I didn't have to test myself.

HERMAN.   You'd've passed. You'd've done your utmost. Like when you had to see Miriam suffer ... and when you helped me find the strength to do my utmost too ... and if I never thanked you for that, I thank you now, from the bottom of my heart.

CHRISTINE.   You helped me just as much, or more. When Moe died you were my manly shoulder to lean on, my Rock of Gibraltar.

HERMAN.   *(After a pause.)* Christine, if you didn't throw it out, might I trouble you for a Diet Pepsi?

CHRISTINE.   Do I ever deny you anything? *(She goes to refrigerator, gets and opens a bottle of Diet Pepsi, gives it to Herman, as movers return.)* I'll get you a clean and alluring paper cup. *(She ascends to entry hall, as Ralph goes to the table in it, tells Chuck.)*

RALPH.   We'll put this by the elevator.

CHRISTINE.   Oops! Wait a second! *(Crossing to table.)* I almost let you take away my airplane ticket. *(She opens table's drawer, removes an airline envelope, goes to bookcase, sets envelope on a shelf, during:)*

HERMAN.   It might've been just as well. Today's weather

forecast is another blinding snowstorm.

RALPH.   No it isn't.

HERMAN.   Yes it is. *(Christine exits to kitchen wing. Movers pick up table, carry it out. Herman sets beverage bottle on floor, rises, runs over, snatches airline envelope, sticks it in his inner jacket pocket, then he runs back, resumes his seat. Movers return, descend to living room.)*

RALPH.   *(To Herman.)* Please get up. We need to take that chair.

HERMAN.   *(Rising.)* Ralph, Chuck ... six hundred bucks. Apiece.

CHUCK.   Ralph.

RALPH.   What?

CHUCK.   That's a lot of money.

RALPH.   I thought you want to go to Florida.

CHUCK.   I do — but this way I won't have to go in a truck.

RALPH.   *(To Herman.)* Why is it so important to you to keep our client in New York?

HERMAN.   I'm worried about her health. The climate in Florida is too moist for her. She has a serious sinus condition. *(Christine returns with a paper cup, descends to living room.)*

CHRISTINE.   All the clean cups are gone. I had to rinse out a used one.

RALPH.   Mrs. Millman.

CHRISTINE.   Yes, Ralph?

RALPH.   How's your sinus condition?

CHRISTINE.   It's fine. Probably because I don't have one. *(Ralph looks at Herman, for several seconds, then turns to Chuck.)*

RALPH.   Shall we take the chair? *(Movers lift armchair, carry it to entry hall, exit, as Herman picks up bottle of Diet Pepsi, sits on sofa. Christine crosses to him.)*

CHRISTINE.   Did it have time to breathe?

HERMAN.   Yes.

CHRISTINE.   I wish I were as lucky. *(She hands him cup; he fills it with cola, sets bottle on floor, drinks.)* Herman, if it's any consolation to you, I have certain areas of disappointment in my children too.

HERMAN.   I thought they're both very devoted to you.

CHRISTINE.    They are. They call me every day, they invite me on all their family vacations, they never let me be alone on major holidays, and they have lunch with me once a week.

HERMAN.    So far I fail to see your grounds for disappointment.

CHRISTINE.    They're just going through the motions. For example, when they invite me on vacations, I politely refuse, so they can have their privacy. They never coax me, and my feeling is:  If they weren't sure I'd say no they wouldn't ask me.

HERMAN.    Did you ever say that, at any of your lunches with them?

CHRISTINE.    It's never with *them*. It's always with *one* of them. And it's never the same one twice in a row. My feeling is they decided to rotate — first you, then me — we'll take turns at who has to kill a few hours with the old lady.

HERMAN.    *(After sipping cola.)*   I notice you keep using the term "my feeling is." But a feeling isn't a fact, it's only a feeling. You should talk this over with them, and try to clear the air.

CHRISTINE.    I should, I know I should, but I'm afraid to criticize them.

HERMAN.    Why?

CHRISTINE.    They might stop going through the motions. *(Herman drains cup, puts it on floor.)*

HERMAN.    My advice is don't be afraid. Don't be afraid of anything.

CHRISTINE.    That's good advice, but it's hard to follow.

HERMAN.    Try. Don't give up. Don't run away from life to hide out with another widow who's got a personality that I predict within six months will drive you crazy.

CHRISTINE.    Herman, you don't understand. *(She picks up empty cup and bottle, sets them on mantel, faces Herman.)* You're not a widow. You're a widower. There's a big difference. When you go to a dinner party, an extra man, *any* man, is a blue chip stock. But when I go to a dinner party, an extra woman, *any* woman, is a charity case. And when the party's over, you leave, no problem. But before *I* can leave, I have to convince my host he doesn't need to take me home. Then, if I can't find a cab, and there's no bus in sight, I walk ... alone ... terrified ... and even worse, I know just how alone I really am.

HERMAN.    I don't get invited to that many dinner parties.

CHRISTINE.    You would be if you wanted to.

HERMAN.    Maybe, maybe not. Sometimes my personality drives people crazy too. True or false? *(Christine wiggles one hand, palm down, meaning "maybe yes, maybe no.")* Miriam used to tell me I have a tendency to be abrasive, and my inner charm would shine through stronger if I was more low-keyed. I guess that also was good advice, but I never took it. *(Christine sits on sofa.)* Looking back, on some occasions my wife was wiser than I gave her credit for.

CHRISTINE.    Why do you have to say "on some occasions?" Why must your infrequent praise of Miriam always be watered down?

HERMAN.    I retract the statement. My wife was wiser than I gave her credit for on *many* occasions.

CHRISTINE.    How about on *most* occasions, or on *all* occasions?

HERMAN.    Not all. There's a thin line between watering down and flooding the market.

CHRISTINE.    You and I have different standards. Miriam was my dearest friend; I revere her memory.

HERMAN.    Maybe you revere it too much. Moe was *my* dearest friend, but that doesn't mean I'm blind to the faults he had.

CHRISTINE.    Neither am I.

HERMAN.    For instance, he was very stubborn.

CHRISTINE.    Moe? When and where was he stubborn?

HERMAN.    Always, in business. Once he decided what the deal should be, that was it, take it or leave it, no negotiating.

CHRISTINE.    What's wrong with driving a hard bargain?

HERMAN.    Nothing. But when a man makes a coat for three thousand dollars, and wants to sell it for twelve, and he's offered eleven-five but he won't accept it — in some circles that man is considered too inflexible.

CHRISTINE. *(Checking wristwatch.)* I hope I won't be late for brunch. At Paul and Barbara's. They're gathering the entire family. Paul said they'll get me so drunk I'll tell the pilot to move over and let me fly the plane.

HERMAN. But *outside* of business, and this was another fault he had, he was too flexible. He accepted anything and everything that came his way, and whatever his own private emotions were, he never let them show.

CHRISTINE. In other words, he never lost his cool.

HERMAN. That's correct.

CHRISTINE. Then why did you say, yesterday, in this very room, his finest quality was his warmth?

HERMAN. It was. But he *used* his warmth, and his cheerful happy-go-lucky disposition, as a method of avoiding arguments.

CHRISTINE. *(Rising.)* Excuse me. *(She goes to bar, eats a chocolate.)*

HERMAN. What's the matter? Is the truth so bitter that you have to sweeten it?

CHRISTINE. Herman, I think it's time for you to leave. Disloyalty to friends is *nobody's* finest quality.

HERMAN. Neither is refusing to admit the truth. *(Christine faces him, and erupts in anger.)*

CHRISTINE. It's not the truth! The truth is I loved him, and I miss him, and you have no right to insult him, because he was a better man than you are!

HERMAN. I never said he wasn't.

CHRISTINE. Will you please leave? Will you please, please leave?

HERMAN. Not yet. *(He rises, crosses to her, and his anger erupts.)* How the hell can you accuse me of disloyalty to Moe? I loved him too, and in my own way I miss him just as goddamn much as you do! And who the hell are you to make me defend my love for Miriam? I loved Miriam before you even met her. I was married to her for thirty-eight years, and in all those years not a day went by that I didn't realize how lucky I was that she loved *me*, and she put up with me, and improved me, and inspired me, because she had more faith in me than I did! *(Silence, then anger drains, for each of them.)*

I apologize.

CHRISTINE.   So do I.

HERMAN.   I should've hit a tender nerve more tenderly.

CHRISTINE.   It's more important that you hit it accurately. *(She sits on the sofa.)* At work Moe was too inflexible, at home he was too flexible. He always deferred to whatever I wanted. That made me feel I always had to be right — and that's a heavy burden. But my husband liked to be a martyr, and sacrifice his needs for mine, as if I didn't need to understand his needs, and try to fulfill them. So in a way ... my needs meant less to him than his needs ... so at the same time he was being generous he was being selfish. *(Beat.)* Does that make sense to you?

HERMAN.   Not completely. Could you say it again?

CHRISTINE.   No. I'm surprised I could even say it once.

HERMAN.   *(Sitting beside her.)* You know what I'd like to do?

CHRISTINE.   Now?

HERMAN.   No. Tonight, when I'm alone in my apartment.

CHRISTINE.   What would you like to do?

HERMAN.   I'd like to talk to my wife. For thirty seconds. That's all, just thirty seconds.

CHRISTINE.   What would you say?

HERMAN.   I'd ask her where she put my sterling silver fountain pen. I've been looking for it three years, but I can't find it.

CHRISTINE.   I'd like to talk to my husband for thirty seconds too. I'd like to ask him how he thinks I'll do living with Beverly Siegel.

HERMAN.   I'd like to talk with Miriam thirty seconds every day.

CHRISTINE.   Me too. I mean with Moe.

HERMAN.   But the most important thing I'd say is: "Did I make you happy? Are you glad you spent your life with me? Was I worthy of you?"

CHRISTINE.   *(Touching his cheek.)* She'd say yes. Believe me, she'd say yes.

HERMAN.   What's the most important thing you'd say to Moe?

CHRISTINE.   I'd tell him I forgive him.

HERMAN.   For what?

CHRISTINE.   For leaving me before I had a chance to say good-bye to him, to let him know how much I cherished him.

HERMAN.   *(Touching her cheek.)* He knew. Believe me, he knew. *(Ralph returns.)*

RALPH.   Mrs. Millman, will you please check the bedrooms to make sure we took everything we were supposed to? *(Christine rises, exits, as Herman asks Ralph.)*

HERMAN.   Where's Chuck?

RALPH.   He's busy working — but he sends his love to you. *(Ralph crosses to ottoman, picks up Herman's overcoat, carefully folds it, puts Herman's muffler, hat, and gloves on top of it, then he hurls all items into the air, and they fall to floor.)*

HERMAN.   Ralph, I'm going to ignore that ... in favor of: · *(He raises eight fingers.)* Eight hundred bucks for you, eight hundred for Chuck. That's my final offer. *(Lowering fingers.)* Well, what do you say?

RALPH.   I say, and I also speak for my associate ... *(He brandishes one finger, the one used to "give the finger.")*

HERMAN.   Forget it. One thousand is out of the question.

RALPH.   In that case kindly help me roll up the rug. *(They roll up the area rug, with equal proficiency, during:)*

HERMAN.   I hope you notice this is a top-quality piece of merchandise. I sold it to her, at cost plus zero percent. I'm in the carpet business. That's why I can do this just as well as you can.

RALPH.   *(Rolling task completed.)* Now let's see how you carry it to the entry hall. *(They lift rug, carry it to entry, Ralph with minimal effort, Herman struggling. They set rug on floor near door, as Christine returns.)*

CHRISTINE.   All clear. Everything gone except my luggage.

RALPH.   *(Crossing to ottoman.)* Then we're almost finished. *(Lifting ottoman, ascending to entry.)* Unless you'd like us to load Mr. Lewis. *(Ralph exits. Christine and Herman descend to living room, where she gazes around.)*

CHRISTINE.   It looks so different. It looks so empty. It used to be a home, now it's just ... a place. *(Herman picks up items*

*Ralph threw, puts on his muffler and overcoat.)* Why don't you come to Paul and Barbara's with me? I'm sure you'll be more than welcome.

HERMAN. I can't. It's a work day, and I have to work. Thanks for the coffee, the doughnut, and the Diet Pepsi.

CHRISTINE. Thanks for the candy, and the lovely poem that went with it.

HERMAN. But most of all, thanks for the past ... *(Checking wristwatch.)* eighteen hours.

CHRISTINE. My pleasure. They were wonderful. Weird, but wonderful.

HERMAN. By the way, what you said last night was true.

CHRISTINE. What I said about what?

HERMAN. Before yesterday I *did* neglect you. My only excuse is that even if I didn't see you, I knew you were just a taxi ride away, and that you and I were still ... I don't know ... *(Touching her hand.)* connected. *(Ralph and Chuck return.)*

RALPH. Mrs. Millman, we'll load the sofa, make sure everything's tied down good and tight, then we'll come back for the rug and you can sign our work sheet.

CHRISTINE. You did a great job. You're two terrific fellas.

RALPH. Thank you. You're a very lovely lady. *(Beat.)* So I think you should know that Mr. Lewis tried to bribe me and Chuck eight hundred bucks apiece to walk off the job.

CHUCK. *(Shocked.) Eight* hundred? He upped it to eight?

RALPH. You said no. Your integrity is not for sale. *(He indicates sofa. He and Chuck lift it, carry it out, during:)*

CHUCK. When did I say that?

RALPH. In the truck. But you said it very softly, so maybe you didn't hear. *(Movers exit.)*

CHRISTINE. Why? Wouldn't Mayflower send me *other* movers?

HERMAN. Yes, but probably not till Monday. So I'd have all weekend to postpone what now appears to be the inevitable. *(Kissing her cheek.)* Goodbye, Christine. Keep well.

CHRISTINE. You too. *(He ascends to entry hall.)*

HERMAN. You'll be glad to hear the *real* weather forecast is fair and warmer. *(He exits. Christine waits for him to return. When he doesn't, she gets cup and bottle from the mantel, exits to kitchen wing. Herman appears in open doorway, sees room empty, then rings chimes. Christine hurries back.)* I remembered something I forgot. *(He reaches into his inner jacket pocket, removes airline envelope.)* I inadvertently stole your plane ticket. *(He gives her the envelope. She puts it on a bookcase shelf, during:)*

CHRISTINE.   How would that stop me? I'd say I lost it, and if they didn't replace it I'd buy another one.

HERMAN.   Christine, don't be logical. I was clutching at straws. And since that was my last straw … it looks like you're moving to Florida. *(She sits on steps to entry hall.)*

CHRISTINE.   Sit down and keep me company till Ralph and Chuck get back. *(He sits beside her.)* Maybe sometime you'll fly down and let me take you to dinner at La Miami Raisinette.

HERMAN.   Would Beverly come with us?

CHRISTINE.   No. She might try to seduce you.

HERMAN.   She already did. Last year she sent me a Chanukah card with a picture of her in a bathing suit.

CHRISTINE.   See? What did I tell you? You're a blue chip stock.

HERMAN.   The problem is I already offered my heart to someone else. But she won't accept it. *(Reaching into another jacket pocket.)* So I better give her her plane ticket. *(He takes out the actual ticket.)* What I gave you before was just the envelope. *(He gives her the ticket. She rises, crosses to bookcase, puts ticket in its envelope, during:)*

CHRISTINE.   Herman, please. Come to brunch with me and my family.

HERMAN.   No. I don't want to share you with your family. I want you all to myself. *(She resumes her seat on steps.)*

CHRISTINE.   So what do you say? Will you fly down and have dinner with me?

HERMAN.   Yes.

CHRISTINE.   Good. Let's make it … three weeks from tomorrow.

HERMAN.   Sounds fine. When I get to my office I'll check my date book.

CHRISTINE.   Of course you could fly down with me *today*, so I'd have a hand to cling to during take-off and landing.

HERMAN.    Your flight's at five-fifteen. At six o'clock I've got an appointment for a haircut.

CHRISTINE.    Herman, did anybody ever call you an incurable romantic?

HERMAN.    No, you're the first. *(Silence, broken by:)*

CHRISTINE.    Do you really think I'm running away to hide?

HERMAN.    Do you?

CHRISTINE.    No. Maybe. Not necessarily. But if I *am* hiding, what am I hiding from?

HERMAN.    I wouldn't presume to answer that. You have to do it for yourself.

CHRISTINE.    Aw, come on, presume. Don't always be so namby-pamby.

HERMAN.    I can't help it. That's my biggest fault.

CHRISTINE.    I think I'm running away from decorating the same apartments for the same clients, from blinding snowstorms, from being in a rut. I think I'm looking for new challenges, new adventures.

HERMAN.    Well, if that's what you think, then that's what you think.

CHRISTINE.    Unless I'm kidding myself. Unless the only thing I'm really changing is the scenery.

HERMAN.    I could help you. And at the same time help myself.

CHRISTINE.    How?

HERMAN.    I could fill your life with love, and let you do the same for me.

CHRISTINE.    On second thought, can we make our dinner date *two* weeks from tomorrow?

HERMAN.    I'll go check my date book. *(He rises, then she does.)* Be happy, Christine. Look to the future, not to the past.

CHRISTINE.    I'll try.

HERMAN.    So will I. Because Moe and Miriam are dead. They're dead. And if you and I go around acting like that when we lost them we lost everything, then we might as well be dead too. *(He starts to leave.)*

CHRISTINE.    Herman, wait. There's something I'd like you

61

to do for me.

HERMAN. *(Turning back.)* What?

CHRISTINE. *(Matter of factly.)* Marry me. *(She kneels on both knees, spreads her arms, implores.)* Fill my life with love ... and let me do the same for you. *(Herman reacts astonished, for several seconds, then.)*

HERMAN. This is so sudden. *(He kneels facing her, takes her hands.)* What finally brought you to your senses?

CHRISTINE. Well, I didn't make a list, but.... Number one: Every time you walk out the door I hope you come back. Number two: If you're crazy enough to think an old zircon is a precious ruby, I'd be crazy to let you get away from me. *(He stands, helps her to her feet, takes off muffler and overcoat, puts them on fireplace hearth, during:)*

HERMAN. If your heart's really set on living in Florida, we can.

CHRISTINE. Do you think you could be happy there?

HERMAN. No. My business is established here, and it's too risky for me to change accountants. *(Movers return, Ralph holding a work sheet attached to a clipboard. Chuck enthuses.)*

CHUCK. All systems go. Onward to Florida.

HERMAN. *(To Christine.)* Do you want to tell them or should I?

CHRISTINE. I will. *(Crossing to movers.)* Ralph. *(Ralph writes on work sheet, gives Christine pen and clipboard.)*

RALPH. Okay, Mrs. Millman, just sign on the dotted line.

HERMAN. Christine, may I please see that? I want to make sure Ralph didn't, shall we say, put a few extra petals on the Mayflower. *(He takes clipboard, scans the figures on work sheet.)*

RALPH. I didn't — and I resent the accusation.

CHRISTINE. Ralph, Chuck, there's been a little change of plans. Please put *all* my things in storage. I'm not moving to Florida.

HERMAN. *(Handing Christine board.)* You can sign. When the bill comes I'll study it with a fine-tooth comb, but at a moment like this I won't split hairs.

CHUCK. A moment like what?

CHRISTINE.    Mr. Lewis and I have decided to get married.
RALPH.    *(Incredulously.)* To each other?
HERMAN.    You seem surprised.
RALPH.    I'm speechless. *(To Christine.)* Why?
CHRISTINE.    We're young, and we're in love. *(She signs work sheet, gives pen and clipboard to Ralph.)*
CHUCK.    Nice work, Ralph. I'm not going to Florida, and I blew eight hundred bucks.
RALPH.    Chuck, quit whining. Just congratulate the bride.
CHUCK.    Congratulations, Mrs. Millman.
RALPH.    Mrs. Millman, if you played your cards right you could've had *me* ... but congratulations, and best wishes. *(He kisses Christine's hand, then slaps a carbon of work sheet into Herman's.)* You too. *(Movers pick up rolled rug, exit, as Herman calls.)*
HERMAN.    Ralph, I'll give you a call. We'll have lunch sometime. *(Herman closes door, puts work sheet on a bookcase shelf.)* Do you want a big wedding or a small one?
CHRISTINE.    Small. What do you want?
HERMAN.    Small. Maybe Steven will fly in with Josh and Jenny.
CHRISTINE.    If I can tear you away from work, we'll call him from Paul and Barbara's.
HERMAN.    After we revive all those who faint.
CHRISTINE.    But first I'll call Bev. I'll say ... I'll say ... on second thought I'll send Bev a telegram.
HERMAN.    *I'll* call Bev. With you beside me I can conquer anything. *(Taking her hands.)* Will we live in my apartment? Redecorated within reason?
CHRISTINE.    I think I'd rather make a fresh start somewhere else.
HERMAN.    I think so would I.
CHRISTINE.    Meanwhile I'll stay in a hotel.
HERMAN.    This afternoon I'll help you find one and check in. *(Beat.)* Then we can give each other a free engagement gift. Unless you want to pretend that last night never happened, and wait until our wedding night.
CHRISTINE.    No. I want to start practicing for perfect.

Besides ... *(A confession.)* I didn't wait until my wedding night the first time either.
HERMAN.  I know. Moe told me. *(They kiss.)*

## THE CURTAIN FALLS

# PROPERTY LIST

Sheet of paper with list (HERMAN)
Reading glasses (HERMAN)
Mayflower book cartoons (empty) (RALPH, CHUCK)
Sheaf of wrapping paper (RALPH)
Compact disks (CHUCK)
Dish of chocolates (CHRISTINE)
Three sample carpet swatches (CHRISTINE)
Beverage bottles (CHRISTINE)
Drinking glasses (CHRISTINE)
Can of soda (CHRISTINE)
Art book (CHRISTINE)
Mayflower book cartons, sealed
Mayflower wardrobe cartons, sealed, with dresses
Purse (CHRISTINE)
Keys (CHRISTINE)
2 bottles of sherry (CHRISTINE)
Cordial glasses for sherry (CHRISTINE)
Checkbook with checks (CHRISTINE)
Pen (CHRISTINE)
King size box spring (CHUCK, RALPH)
Mattress (CHUCK, RALPH)
5 pound gift-wrapped box of chocolates, with card (HERMAN)
Metal bed frame (CHUCK, RALPH)
Kitchen counter breadboard (CHRISTINE) with:
  3 paper cups with coffee
  paper napkins
  2 doughnuts
Bottle of Diet Pepsi (CHRISTINE)
Airline ticket envelope, with ticket (CHRISTINE)
Paper cup (CHRISTINE)
Clipboard with worksheet (RALPH)
Pen (RALPH)

# COSTUME PLOT

## ACT ONE

**CHRISTINE**

Rust-colored silk blouse
Brown/black silk trousers
Black underbody suit
Brown suede loafers
Brown/orange head scarf
Stockings
Gold wedding and engagement bands
Blue-patterned kimono
Lavender slippers
Black evening cocktail dress
Black satin shoes
Diamond and pearl earrings
Blacklama fur coat
Black evening bag

**HERMAN**

Wool overcoat with mink lining
Green hat with fur lining
Wool knit scarf
Black leather gloves
Green wool cardigan sweater
Brown wool trousers
Beige shirt
Brown-striped tie
Brown shoes with gum soles
Black socks
Brown-stripe suspenders
T-shirt and shorts underwear
Gold wedding ring
2-piece pin stripe suit
White shirt with French cuffs
Navy suspenders
Gold cuff links

Wine and gold-patterned tie
Black tie shoes
Navy Chesterfield overcoat
Navy Homberg hat

**CHUCK**
Mayflower moving company uniform
Red bandanna (for head)
High-top sneakers
Plaid jacket

**RALPH**
Mayflower moving company uniform
Brown leather work boots
Brown cowboy belt
Yankees baseball cap

## ACT TWO

**CHRISTINE**
Cinnamon silk blouse
Beige wool crepe trousers
Brown belt with gold buckle
Dark brown pump shoes
Flesh-colored underbody suit
Gold earrings
Gold jacket pin
Pearl necklace
Brown leather handbag

**HERMAN**
Gray corduroy shorts jacket
Brown wool trousers
Blue shirt
Blue-striped tie
Gray/brown suspenders
Brown shoes with gum soles

# SOUND EFFECTS

Entry hall intercom buzzer
Door chimes

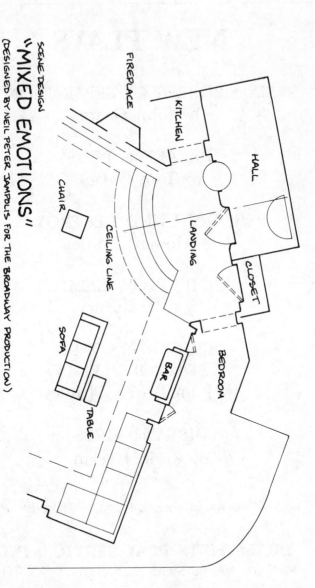

SCENE DESIGN
"MIXED EMOTIONS"
(DESIGNED BY NEIL PETER JAMPOLIS FOR THE BROADWAY PRODUCTION)

FIREPLACE

KITCHEN

HALL

CHAIR

CEILING LINE

LANDING

CLOSET

SOFA

TABLE

BAR

BEDROOM

# NEW PLAYS

SIX DEGREES OF SEPARATION
by John Guare

BREAKING LEGS
by Tom Dulack

SEARCH AND DESTROY
by Howard Korder

THE SNOW BALL
by A.R. Gurney

BEGGARS IN THE
HOUSE OF PLENTY
by John Patrick Shanley

DISTANT FIRES
by Kevin Heelan

*Write for information as to availability*

**DRAMATISTS PLAY SERVICE, INC.**
440 Park Avenue South     New York, N.Y. 10016